AN OPEN INTELLIGENT INFORMATION SYSTEMS ARCHITECTURE

About the Author

Dr. Rajeev Kaula is a Gold Medalist and a specialist in Artificial Intelligence. He had obtained M.S. in Information Systems from Roosevelt University, Chicago (USA) after having got M.M.S. from Banaras Hindu University. He obtained Ph.D from Watson School of Engineering and School of Management, University of New York at Binghamton, New York (USA).

Dr. Kaula is an Associate Professor of Computer Information Systems at South-west Missouri State University, Springfield, Missouri (USA). His major areas of research include open information systems, knowledge based systems, distributed decision support systems, object-oriented analysis, computer integrated manufacturing and information engineering. Dr. Kaula has published numerous papers in reputed journals on the above topics in information systems. He has also served as a reviewer for major journals and publishers in the field of information systems.

AN OPEN INTELLIGENT INFORMATON SYSTEMS ARCHITECTURE

RAJEEV KAULA
M.S. Information Systems, Roosevelt University,
Ph.D., State University of New York

CONCEPT PUBLISHING COMPANY, NEW DELHI - 110059

ISBN 81-7022-722-4

First Published 1999

Published and Printed by

Ashok Kumar Mittal

Concept Publishing Company,

A/15-16, Commercial Block, Mohan Garden,
NEW DELHI - 110059

Phone: 5648039, 5649024
Fax : 091-(11)-5648053

DEDICATED

TO

MY BELOVED PARENTS

Prof. P.N. Kaula and **Mrs. Asha Kaula**

PREFACE

The conventional wisdom in intelligent information processing system development is that systems should be developed with global consistency and completeness. This viewpoint has increased the complexity of systems development. Hewitt and deJong (1984) suggested an alternative approach for intelligent systems development called the open-systems approach. The open-systems approach envisages intelligent systems consisting of many small autonomous intelligent subsystems which cooperate by communicating with each other during problem solving. In such an environment there is no global schema, consistency or completeness. However, existing information processing conceptual architecture like composite database, federated database, production systems and blackboard systems architectures have limitations in their use toward realizing open intelligent information systems.

The study proposes a new conceptual architecture called an Open Intelligent Information Systems (OIIS) architecture for the design of open intelligent information systems. The architecture has many components. First there is a user interface through which the user interacts with the system. Secondly there is the provision for multiple autonomous intelligent subsystems. Thirdly there is a concept dictionary, which provides an index of specific knowledge handled by various autonomous intelligent subsystems. The mode of communication within the OIIS is based on the speech act theory of language proposed by Searle (1969). However, speech acts have been modified and called message acts, and implemented in the communications dictionary component. Autonomous intelligent subsystems directly communicate with each other using message acts (communications dictionary) after making inquiries to the concept dictionary during problem solving. A business application prototype is developed in the Prolog language to test the architecture's working.

The development of the OIIS architecture in this work has major implications for the future development of intelligent systems, apart from providing new directions for further research.

RAJEEV KAULA

CONTENTS

Preface 7

Chapter 1: Introduction **13-21**

1.1 The promise of fifth generation infomation processing *15*
1.1.1 Intelligent Information System Development *15*
1.2 Limitations of Existing Approaches *17*
1.2.1 Limitations of Conventional Approaches *17*
1.2.1.1 Information Representation *17*
1.2.1.2 Solutions in Situations of Uncertainty *17*
1.2.1.3 Reasoning Facility *18*
1.2.2 Limitations of the Fifth Generation Approaches *18*
1.3 The Promise of Open-Systems *19*
1.4 The Objective of this Research *19*
1.5 Outline of the Study *20*

Chapter 2: The Evolution of Information Processing System Components **22-41**

2.1 Information Systems *23*
2.1.1 Types of Information Systems in Organizations *23*
2.1.2 Information System Development Methodologies *25*
2.1.3 Conceptual Primitives of Information Systems *25*
2.2 Knowledge Systems *28*
2.2.1 Distinguishing Characteristics of Knowledge Systems *29*
2.2.2 Organizational Requirements for Knowledge Systems *30*
2.2.3 Conceptual Primitives of Knowledge Systems *31*
2.2.4 Inference Engine Strategies *32*
2.2.4.1 Generate and test *33*
2.2.4.2 Hill Climbing *33*
2.2.4.3 Breadth first search *33*
2.2.4.4 Best-first search *33*
2.2.5 Knowledge Representation and Acquisition *34*
2.3 Neural Network Systems *35*

2.3.1 Structure of Neurons and Neural Systems *35*
2.3.2 Evolution of Neural Systems *36*
2.4 Summary of Advances and Unresolved Issues *37*
2.4.1 Impact on Organizations *37*
2.4.2 Advances and Limitations of Information Systems *39*
2.4.3 Advances and Limitations of Knowledge Systems *40*
2.4.4 Limitations of Neural Network Systems *41*

Chapter 3: Review of Information Processing Conceptual Architecture **42-59**

3.1 Data-based Architectures *43*
3.1.1 File-Centered Architectures *43*
3.1.2 Database-centered Architecture *44*
3.1.3 Distributed Database-Centerd Architectures *46*
3.1.3.1 Composite Database Architectures *48*
3.1.3.2 Federated Database Architectures *49*
3.2 Knowledge-based Architectures *50*
3.2.1 Production Systems *50*
3.2.1.1 Knowledge Base Structure *51*
3.2.1.2 Inference Engine Structure *52*
3.2.1.3 User Interface *52*
3.2.2 Blackboard Systems *53*
3.2.2.1 Distributed Problem Solving Characteristics *53*
3.2.2.2 Blackboard Architecture Components *54*
3.3 Limitations of Current Architectures *56*
3.3.1 Limitations of File-centered Architectures *56*
3.3.2 Limitations of Database-centered Architectures *57*
3.3.3 Limitations of Production Systems Architecture *58*
3.3.4 Limitations of Blackboard Systems Architecture *58*

Chapter 4: An Open Intelligent Information Systems Architecture **60-75**

4.1 Open-Systems Approach Characteristics *60*
4.1.1 Properties of Open-Systems *61*
4.1.1.1 Continuous Change and Evolution *61*
4.1.1.2 Arm's length Relationships and Decentralized Decision-making *61*
4.1.1.3 Perpetual Inconsistency among knowledge Bases *61*
4.1.1.4 Need for Negotiation among System Components *61*

4.1.1.5 Inadequacy of the closed-world Assumption *62*
4.1.2 Distributed Problem Solving and Open-Systems Approach *62*
4.1.2.1 Direct Communication *63*
4.1.2.2 Broadcast Communication *63*
4.1.2.3 Indirect Communication *63*
4.1.3 Elements of an Open-Systems Architecture *64*
4.2 Conceptual Design of the OIIS Architecture *66*
4.2.1 Fundamentals of the Architecture *67*
4.2.2 Theoretical Foundations for Communication in OIIS *69*
4.2.3 Syntax and Semantics for Communication in OIIS *72*
4.3 Discussion of Key Advances *74*

Chapter 5: OIIS Architecture Implementation **76-90**

5.1 Description of the OIIS Case Study *76*
5.1.1 Overview of the Case *76*
5.1.2 Operational Details of the Case *77*
5.2 Description of the OIIS Architecture Details *84*
5.2.1 Structure of Concept Dictionary *84*
5.2.2 Structure of Communication Dictionary *85*
5.2.3 Structure of Inference Engine *87*
5.2.3.1 Reasons for New Inference Control Strategy *88*
5.2.3.2 Development of New Inference Engine *89*
5.3 Summary and Conclusions *90*

Chapter 6: Contributions of the Research **91-95**

6.1 Contributions to Information Processing System Theory and Practice *91*
6.1.1 Open-World system Development *91*
6.1.2 Operationalization of Speech Acts *92*
6.1.3 Relevancy of Conceptual Architectures *92*
6.1.4 Modularization of Intelligent Information systems *92*
6.1.5 Integrate Existing Intelligent systems within open-world Environment *93*
6.2 Implications for Further Research *93*
6.2.1 Open-systems Development Methodology *93*
6.2.2 Open-systems Development Life-Cycle *93*
6.2.3 Machine Learning Mechanisms for Open-Systems *94*

6.2.4 Usage of other Language Constructs *94*
6.2.5 Usage of Varied Knowledge Representation Schemes *94*
6.2.6 Handling of Uncertainity *94*
6.3 Conclusions *95*

Appendices

A. Communication Dictionary Entries 96-103
B. OIIS Architecture 104-117
C. OIIS Inference Engine Initiation 118-131
D. Student Advising System 132-138

Bibliography 139-149
Index 150-151

1

INTRODUCTION

Computerized information processing is providing the basis for a new revolution toward which societies are being compelled to move--called as information revolution. After decades of computer evolution, information processing systems are becoming an accepted factor in the success of societies. Since the development of the first computer in the late 1940's, four generations of information processing systems have evolved which have transformed the way computers are used. Currently the fourth generation is in vogue and tentative forays are being made toward the full realization of the power of fifth generation computer systems.

These developments in information processing systems have been and continue to be influenced by many factors, including an organization's environment, the methodology used, the type of language, and implementation issues. Implicit in the development of any information processing system is the role of the conceptual architecture which provides the framework for integrating the basic conceptual components of the system for problem solving [Martin, 1983; Harmon & King, 1985; Bubenko, 1986; Waterman, 1986]. Since the first application of computers in organizations began in 1954 [Davis & Olson, 1985], all types of information processing systems have been based on some conceptual architecture. These architectures, which are independent of language, software, methodology and implementation issues, provide a framework by which the primitive system representation components can be integrated for system building and problem solving.

Consequently the way an information processing system is perceived, described and specified conceptually largely follows the way compatible conceptual architectures have evolved [Bubenko, 1986]. The earlier view of using data-based conceptual architectures for problem solving has now been gradually augmented by knowledge-based conceptual architectures (variably referred to as expert systems, knowledge systems or intelligent information systems).

Such intelligent information systems development is the main concern of the fifth generation information processing and a related concern of this thesis. However, despite the promise of intelligent information systems, there are still problems and bottlenecks hindering their complete realization. In order to alleviate some of the existing bottlenecks of intelligent information systems an alternative approach toward developing such systems is proposed by two researchers C. Hewitt and P. de Jong, which is known as the *open-systems* approach [Hewitt & de Jong, 1983, 1984; Bubenko, 1986]. This dissertation is an attempt to conceptually operationalize intelligent information systems based on the open-systems approach.

The work reported in this dissertation is motivated by the following conjectures:

1. The open-systems view offers sufficient promise to be considered as a credible alternative to intelligent systems development.
2. There does not exist any guidance whatsoever on the way such systems could be fully realized for problem solving. There is no compatible conceptual architecture proposed/suggested that would enable the realization of open intelligent information systems.
3. Existing information processing conceptual architectures have limitations in their use for open intelligent information systems.

In the light of these conjectures, it seems appropriate that efforts should be made toward developing a suitable conceptual architecture for open intelligent information systems. Such a conceptual architecture could then form the basis for a better realization of the promise of fifth generation information processing as well as open intelligent information systems. This dissertation proposes a conceptual architecture for open-based intelligent information systems.

In this chapter an attempt is made to outline the promise of fifth generation information processing for organizations along with the general limitations of the current approaches that motivate development of intelligent information systems and open intelligent systems. The promise of the 'open system' approach is then described. This section broadly specifies the environment in which open intelligent systems could be made possible. The chapter ends with a synopsis of the research undertaken and an outline of this dissertation.

1.1 THE PROMISE OF FIFTH GENERATION INFORMATION PROCESSING

Developments in the fifth generation information processing techniques have prompted researchers to rethink the ways information processing systems are being developed and used. Fifth generation information processing is based on the use and development of predominantly artificial intelligence techniques and approaches. Artificial intelligence is commonly defined as the effort to develop computer-based systems (both hardware and software) that behave like humans. Such systems, it is felt, should be able to learn natural languages, accomplish coordinated physical tasks (robotics), develop and utilize a perceptual apparatus that informs their physical behaviour and language (visual and oral perception systems), and finally exhibit logic, reasoning and learning capabilities that we associate with human beings [Feigenbaum & Cohen, 1981; Feigenbaum & McCorduck, 1985; Laudon & Laudon, 1988]. No system yet developed comes close to possessing any of these human qualities [Dreyfus, 1979; Schon, 1983; Dreyfus & Dreyfus, 1983; Winograd & Flores, 1987], but the fallout from research on artificial intelligence is having a profound effect on the way information processing systems are being built and developed.

1.1.1 Intelligent Information Systems Development

One major outcome of artificial intelligence research has been the development of knowledge-based information processing systems or intelligent information systems [Bubenko, 1983; Bubenko, 1986; Crawford, 1984; Sibley, 1986; Berztiss, 1986; Carlson, 1988; Belkin *et al.*, 1987]. Intelligent information systems focus on the representation of knowledge of highly limited and specific domains of human experience, and then use this knowledge to arrive at solutions to specific problems or situations. Such types of intelligent information systems have captured the imagination of many groups in our society. With successful applications such as geological prospecting, medical diagnosis, chemical analysis, manufacturing products, this fifth generation technique seems poised to transform the workings of many organizations.

Knowledge of how to manage and solve problems within an organization is an enormously valuable corporate asset. At present, organizational knowledge exists in two forms--in the minds of the organizational management/workers and in the various documents developed by the organization. If this knowledge could be more effectively managed, used, and shared, by developing appropriate intelligent systems, the payoff to the organization could be immense [Paradice & Courtney, 1988].

So, the benefits and promise afforded to organizations by the development and use of such knowledge-based fifth generation systems are extensive. Some of these are the following [Martin & Oxman, 1988; Laudon & Laudon, 1988]:

- To preserve the knowledge that might be lost through the retirement, resignation, or death of an acknowledged expert.
- To clone experts mechanically, so that their knowledge can be used to train and instruct others.
- To store information in an active form--to create a knowledge base that many employees can examine, much like an electronic textbook or manual.
- To create a mechanism that is not subject to human feelings like fatigue and worry. This may be especially useful when jobs may be environmentally, physically, or mentally dangerous to humans. These systems may also be useful advisors in times of crisis.
- To eliminate routine and unsatisfying jobs that are currently held by human beings.
- To improve the quality of decision-making in the organization by giving sound and appropriate advice.

In spite of the many acclaimed benefits afforded by the knowledge-based fifth generation systems, existing systems fall short in fulfulling their promises completely. These systems in their existing state are applicable to limited domains only. They are characterized by a narrow notion of expertise and knowledge, limited language for expressing facts and relations, limited assumptions about problem and solution methods and little knowledge of their own scope. Also, they do not try to deal with the difficult questions of relevance, context and background which are essential in any characterization of human knowledge or expertise [Buchanan, 1982; Winograd & Flores, 1987].

However, the promise displayed by such systems in spite of their associated developmental and philosophical problems has potential strategic importance for organizations. Research should continue for the eventual realization of this promise.

1.2 LIMITATIONS OF EXISTING APPROACHES

The need for developing intelligent information systems as well as open intelligent information systems arises out of the shortcomings in the existing modes of systems development.

1.2.1 Limitations of Conventional Approaches

The shortcomings of the existing conventional approaches to systems development have been instrumental in motivating development and use of intelligent information systems. These shortcomings basically reduce the capabilities of conventional information systems for further problem solving. Some of these major drawbacks are now discussed.

1.2.1.1 Information Representation

Conventional information processing systems normally deal with data in its raw form with not much flexibility afforded in its interpretation. Such systems are further limited due to the nature and type of data that could be represented and analyzed [Negoita, 1985; Walker,1987]. This data is often only a part of the knowledge of an organization and so represents "factual knowledge" only. Organizational knowledge also includes "process knowledge" [Paradice & Courtney, 1988]. Consequently it is more appropriate to store organizational knowledge in a more natural way--data along with its interpretation. Such capabilities are not easily available in conventional approaches/systems.

1.2.1.2 Solutions in Situations of Uncertainty

Although conventional information systems were successful for well-defined and routine-type information processing in organizations, their impact was limited in the non-routine and less-defined types of information processing where decisions were taken in the presence of uncertainty [Martin & Oxman, 1988]. Due to the increasing sophistication of computers, information processing systems are now critically embedded in daily organizational activities, and well integrated with organizational working. The development of systems does require (and benefit from) considerable involvement of the eventual users and other people and often results in considerable changes in the organizations with respect to decision making, planning and work procedures [Lyytinen, 1986; Parker, 1989]. This closeness of systems to the working of organizations necessitates that systems provide solutions even when requirements are less well-defined and uncertain. Intelligent information systems techniques enable the generation of solutions in uncertain situations.

1.2.1.3 Reasoning Facility

As information processing systems in general become more involved with the working of the organizations, techniques are needed that enable systems to explain their rationale for solutions to problems, especially when problems are less well-defined and decisions must be taken in the presence of uncertainty. Conventional information processing systems have problems in providing such a capability [Martin & Oxman, 1988].

1.2.2 Limitations of the Fifth Generation Approach

Even the existing intelligent information system approaches are not without problems. The fundamental problem is how to capture and represent large amounts of knowledge in a manner that permit its effective use in problem solving [Lesser & Corkill, 1981; Huhn, 1987]. Also the methodology for intelligent information systems development is still very primitive and not well-defined. Deep theoretical and philosophical problems surface when knowledge is defined for acquisition and usage [Alty & Coombs, 1980; Aikins, 1983; Belkin *et al.*, 1986; Ngwenyama, 1987].

A major drawback also has been the way intelligent systems are perceived in organizations. Conventionally they have been used for individual/group decision support activity only [Fox, 1983; Sprague & McNurlin, 1986; Henderson, 1987; DeSanctis & Gallupe, 1987; Laudon & Laudon, 1988; Agarwal & Prasad, 1989]. This narrowing of usage and perception has unfairly reduced the promise inherent in such systems for wider applications [Blanning, 1987; Popolizio & Cappelli, 1989].

Thus efforts are necessary to overcome such problems so that the promise inherent in fifth generation systems is fully realized. Utilization of the open-systems approach to developing intelligent information systems provides guidelines toward solving some of these existing problems. The promise of the open-systems approach is now discussed.

1.3 THE PROMISE OF OPEN-SYSTEMS

The tacit assumption made by many conventional and intelligent information processing system development approaches is that the main task is to design one (large) system and to achieve total completeness and consistency. This is probably not the way we should continue to build systems as in most cases we already have reached the complexity barrier. Some researchers [Hewitt & de Jong, 1983,1984], envisage future intelligent information processing systems as consisting of a large number of independently developed systems (perhaps operating at disparate geographical locations), which communicate by passing messages (knowledge, data, information) among themselves during problem solving. Such types of intelligent information processing systems have been termed open-systems.

In the open-systems concept of information processing there is no global conceptual schema. There are no global objects. There is no global consistency. The 'closed world assumption' does not hold--we do not know if certain information or knowledge exists. Each participating system exists with its own 'self knowledge'--its own assumptions, constraints and rules. Also every participating system evolves independently, at times passing portions of its knowledge to other systems, and acquiring, by negotiation, knowledge from its communicating 'partners', in order to solve problems.

Such open information processing systems provide natural modularity to the way systems are built and developed. The overall system is termed 'open' because the various participating systems are independently built and integrated with little difficulty with the other existing systems due to their communicative ability. Such types of systems help reduce the current complexity barrier considerably. It is felt that the development of suitable conceptual architecture to support such open-systems would facilitate the realization of their promise.

1.4 THE OBJECTIVE OF THIS RESEARCH

The objective of this research is to propose a new conceptual architecture for intelligent information systems based on the open-system concept, which I refer to as an *open intelligent information systems architecture*. The underlying promise is to develop intelligent information systems which are inherently modular in structure, by utilizing the speech act theory of language [Searle, 1969] as a mechanism for achieving modularity and integrating this idea with open-system concepts. The primary objectives of the work are as follows:

1. To review the primitive concepts relevant in the building of information processing systems, in order to provide the theoretical groundings for developing the conceptual system architectures.
2. To analyze the various conceptual architectures existing for the development of information processing systems; to identify their limitations for open intelligent systems, in order to focus on the need for a new conceptual architecture which will overcome these shortcomings.
3. To propose the new conceptual architecture (open intelligent information systems architecture), and then specify the key advances brought about by this architecture for systems development.
4. To evaluate the validity of the new architecture by a sample implementation of its structure, and then identify the implications of such an architecture for further research and development.

The research is both qualitative and quantitative. It is qualitative in the sense that it draws heavily on the concepts involved in knowledge systems development and integrates it with the speech act theory of language and open-system concepts. The quantitative part is the actual implementation of the architecture on the computer to improve and justify its existence in operation. The research, contributes to further understanding of the various dimensions involved in intelligent information system development.

1.5 OUTLINE OF THE STUDY

Chapter 2 provides an outline of the evolution of the various concepts involved in the building of information processing systems. Three categories of information processing systems are discussed: information systems, knowledge systems, and neural network systems. Chapter 3 reviews the conceptual architectures existing for information system and knowledge system development, and also identifies their limitations. Chapter 4 gives a description of the issues involved in the open-systems approach and outlines the conceptual architecture for the open intelligent information system. The major advances brought about by this new architecture are then discussed.

Chapter 5 provides the implementation details of the new open intelligent information system architecture on a computer. A prototype is developed from an order processing business situation from [Gane & Sarson, 1979] case is utilized to prove the conceptual validity of the architecture as well as specify some implementation considerations. Conceptual description of a student advising system using the architectural framework of the thesis is also outlined (Appendix-D) as a basis for additional validation. Chapter 6 examines the implications and contributions of this new architecture for information processing system theory and practice, and gives suggestions for further research.

2

THE EVOLUTION OF INFORMATION PROCESSING SYSTEM COMPONENTS

Human beings have always processed information through the medium of their language (signs, notations, etc.). All human activity when represented or implemented through the medium of language involves the processing of information. With the evolution of societies, as organizations developed and began to wield a strong influence over individuals and their environment, the processing of information became more important. It is this processing of information in organizations that forms the underlying theme of any modern information processing system.

Information today is perceived by many people as a corporate or organizational resource of considerable value, which if efficiently and effectively managed has immense strategic value for the organization [Nolan, 1982; Canning, 1984; Ives & Learmonth, 1984; Cash & Konsynski, 1985; Sprague & McNurlin, 1988]. Information processing systems are generally concerned with the ways in which information can be effectively and efficiently tapped and harnessed by the organization.

Although manual processing of information has been going on in organizations since their inception, it is with the advent of computers that this processing of information took on a different role. Computers provided a mechanism that enabled much more efficient and effective processing of information. Three approaches now basically exist in this computerized processing of information:

1. Information Systems.
2. Knowledge Systems or Intelligent Information Systems.
3. Neural Network Systems.

Each of the above approaches are discussed separately in the following sections. The emphasis of the discussion is on the conceptual evolution of the basic system components required for each of the above approaches. The intent of the discussion is to provide an appropriate basis for analyzing the architectural concepts in later chapters. At the end, a summary of the advances to information processing of these approaches are discussed along with the unresolved issues.

2.1 INFORMATION SYSTEMS

The traditional approach to information processing has resulted in the realization of information as a critical and strategic resource for an organization [Nolan, 1982; Porter, 1985]. Improvements in decision making (speed, accuracy, comprehensiveness), serving even higher customer and client expectations, coordinating dispersed groups in an organization, exercising tighter control over personnel and expenditures, and improving an organization's competitiveness are some of the principal rationales for the use of information systems in organizations [Linger & Hevner, 1986; Kesner, 1988]. Due to this strategic and crucial aspect of information systems in organizations, the way in which such systems are organized, developed and used is usually determined by the design and structure of the organization.

Before going into the details of the evolution of the primitive concepts involved in information systems, a brief overview of the types of information systems in existence and their development methodologies is presented. In addition to providing a broad understanding of the extent to which information systems have influenced and permeated organizations, this overview will also provide an understanding of the way information system development is brought about. Emphasis will be on the role and importance of the primitive system components in bringing about any system development.

2.1.1 Types of Information Systems in Organizations

There are various types of information systems currently in existence, viz. Transaction Processing Systems (TPS), Decision Support Systems

(DSS), Management Information Systems (MIS), Office Automation Systems (OAS), and Executive Support Systems (ESS). The classification of information systems into their various types is dependent on the purpose and tasks they are supposed to serve in an organization. Essentially, information systems have been able to do the following tasks [Laudon & Laudon, 1988; Parker, 1989]:

-- Automate the routine processing of transactions in the organization, viz. Transaction Processing Systems (TPS). Such systems normally form the backbone of information processing in the organization.

-- Generate the information necessary from the routine processing of transactions in the organization, viz. Management Information Systems (MIS) [Gorry, 1971]. Such systems serve the functions of planning, controlling and decision-making and are more oriented at the internal environment of the organization.

-- Automate the processing and transferring of documents in the organization, viz. Office Automation Systems (OAS). Such systems affect the flow of communication within the organization, thereby improving the planning and control mechanisms in the organization. This also results in improving and organization's informal information needs.

-- Generate the information necessary to support non-routine decision making, viz. Decision Support Systems (DSS) [Keen, 1976; Keen & Scott-Morton, 1982; Sprague & Carlson, 1982]. These systems draw on both the internal and external environment to generate information. They improve the individual and group decision-making capability which consequently affects the organization's ability to perform its operations and tasks much more effectively.

-- Generate information necessary to support strategic level functions of the organization, viz. Executive Support Systems (ESS) [Rockart, 1982; Keen, 1985]. These systems draw on the external environment to generate information. Such systems affect the development of an organization's strategy and structure, for the achievement of corporate goals.

2.1.2 Information System Development Methodologies

An information systems methodology is a recommended collection of philosophies, phases, procedures, rules, techniques, tools, documentation, management and training for developers of information systems [Maddison *et al.*, 1983]. A similar conceptual view of an information system methodology considers a development methodology as an organized collection of concepts, beliefs, values and normative principles supported by material resources that help a development group to perceive, to generate, to assess, and to carry out in a systematic manner changes in the object system over a set of contexts [Lyytinen, 1986].

There are numerous systems development methodologies that provide an approach by which different types of information systems could be built, like Structured Analysis and Design Technique (SADT) [Ross, 1977], Structured Analysis and Structured Design (SASD) [DeMarco, 1979; Yourdon & Constantine, 1979], Jackson System Development (JSD) [Jackson, 1983], Information Systems Analysis and Construction (ISAC) [Lundeberg *et al*, 1981]. The purpose of all system development methodologies is to aid the system developer in creating the specifications for the information system to be ultimately built. The general focus of system methodologies is to provide various tools and mechanisms that will enable the systems designer to better represent the needs and requirements of the environment in which the system will operate. However any system specification is dependent upon the conceptual primitives for the eventual working of the system as described in the next section.

2.1.3 Conceptual Primitives of Information Systems

Information systems in general consist of a set of *procedures* which process *data* generated in the organization. Such systems are generally formal *systems* as they are based on fixed definitions of data and procedures and so operate in conformity with pre-defined rules that are relatively fixed and not easily changed [Laudon & Laudon, 1988; Parker, 1988].

The specifications for information systems by any development methodology generally indicate how the *data* in the affected environment will be used to generate the information from the system. The approach toward the usage of data is usually some pre-defined rule or set of rules which may be either already operating or be operational in the future. Such rules provide the *procedures* for this specification. Essentially, it is these procedures that enable the interpretation and application of data and finally the working of the information system.

Thus, all methodologies and the systems built by them are

fundamentally based on the amalgamation of two conceptual components [Negoita, 1985; Martin, 1988]:

-- Data
-- Procedures

Different systems have different types of 'data' and 'procedures', depending on the nature of the system to be built. However it is essential to understand how a system's 'data' and 'procedures' can be specified and organized in order to properly understand the eventual system. It is the evolution in the organization of these conceptual entities that provides the eventual evolution in the types of information system usage and development, along with their concomitant conceptual architectures. The evolution in the organization of these conceptual entities will now be discussed.

Data

Data in information systems comprises facts from which conclusions may be drawn. It corresponds to discrete, recorded facts about phenomena from which we gain information about the world [Tsichritzis & Lochovsky, 1982]. In other words data is the raw material that could be further refined, interpreted or transformed to produce information.

During the early years of information systems development, data was organized in *files*. With time various file organizations came into existence specifying different ways of organizing data like sequential files, indexed files, random files and line-sequential files. An information system would then have numerous files depending upon the type and volume of data that was required for processing. Traditional data processing was based on this organization of data in different files.

Organization of data in files led to a lot of problems as information systems grew in size and importance, such as redundancy, integrity and consistency. This gradually brought a shift in the organization of data from files to *databases*. Database theory provided a mechanism by which data could be organized without the problems associated with files. It was also fast and efficient. Different database systems are currently in existence based on the various data models, popular among them being hierarchical, network and relational models.

The importance of organizing data has also grown with time along with the realization of the strategic value of information. It is now felt that the data employed must be compatible with and structured for multiple uses, represented in easily accessible data models, and used with appropriate management controls [Martin & McClure, 1988]. This complex task of managing data throughout the organization has given rise to the discipline of *information engineering*. The primary focus of information engineering is the 'data' that are stored and maintained by databases and the information that is distilled from these data [Martin & Finkelstein, 1981; Macdonald, 1986; Martin & McClure, 1988].

Procedures

Procedures provide a precise specification of processing of an organization's data which thereby enables an information system to eventually perform and generate information [Tsichritzis & Lochovsky, 1982]. These procedures can also be considered as formalized rules that exist within the organization for its operation and so provide a way of specifying the structure and purpose of the information system. These procedures utilize the stored data for generating information.

The way 'procedures' are specified, determines the final outcome of the system. Sometimes even though the system specification requires the inclusion of certain factors in the procedures to properly represent an organization's working, but the limitations of the procedure specification language inhibits this inclusion. In other words, the procedure specification language can prove to be the constraining factor toward a more versatile information system.

In the earlier period of information systems development, procedure specification required for data manipulation and development of system logic was very tedious and unstructured. This increased the complexity of the system by making the system difficult to maintain. To alleviate this complexity, procedure specifications shifted to structured, modular and top-down mechanisms for systems logic representation. Although structured and top-down design approaches did reduce the complexity of the systems development and maintenance, it shall did not ease the task completely. Lately the development of the fourth generation languages has greatly affected the development efforts. These languages, apart from enabling structured and top-down procedure specifications, have also eased the way organization's working details may be eventually specified and manipulated.

The procedure specification in information systems is normally specified in some computer language, such as COBOL, BASIC, PASCAL, SQL and IDEAL. These specifications are language statements that are executed in sequential order and intrinsically represent and provide the logic of the system. Systems logic is the final mapping of the organizations system specification details, which also largely provides the basis for the systems usage in the organization. The development of the systems logic in an efficient manner such that it is flexible and maintainable has long been the thrust of the *software engineering* discipline [Pressman, 1987].

In spite of the tremendous improvements in the specification of procedures (e.g. fourth generation languages) and data organization (e.g. database technology), information systems are still based on the premise of the separation of data and procedures. This restricts the expressive power of conventional information systems, because humans in general process and represent information not by mixing the separate data and procedures, but by having them in one format by virtue of the natural language facility they possess [Tsichritzis & Lochovsky, 1982; Sowa, 1984].

2.2 KNOWLEDGE SYSTEMS

Knowledge systems (KS) are a different class of systems for processing information. They are a branch of artificial intelligence which also has a direct bearing on organizational information processing systems. Knowledge systems are the result of about 30 years of continuous research. Although both information systems and knowledge systems have approximately the same life span, information system were more successful and popular commercially than knowledge system. One reason for the slow emergence of knowledge systems in the commercial environment was the fact that artificial intelligence research dealt with more complex structures of information (knowledge), and its processing, than has been attempted until now.

Before going into the details of the evolution of primitive concepts involved in knowledge systems, a brief overview of the distinguishing characteristics of knowledge systems as compared to conventional information systems is provided. Specific organizational needs and requirements for using knowledge systems are also discussed. This overview will give a broad understanding of the reasons and sophistication of knowledge systems usage, and it will show the relevance of the primitive concepts (disussed later) in any knowledge system development.

2.2.1 Distinguishing Characteristics of Knowledge Systems

The purpose of building a knowledge system is to transfer human knowledge into a computer program so that the program can make decisions within the problem domain and solve problems in a way that would be considered intelligent if done by a human [Waterman, 1986; Weitzel & Kerschberg, 1989]. Now every program within a conventional information system contains some knowledge about some problem. What makes knowledge systems different is that they represent knowledge in a higher-level form of rules and facts, which is closer to the way people think about a problem [Walker, 1987]. A piece of knowledge in the knowledge system consists of some given data together with information on how these data are to be used. This distinguishes it from conventional information systems where data and information on their usage are stored separately. Thus knowledge systems, instead of processing data as a string of bits, process the meaning of data in terms of real world information [Sowa, 1984].

Another important characteristic which distinguishes a knowledge system from a conventional system is the way the knowledge or expertise is stored and processed. The distinctive characteristic of any knowledge system is that its processes are state-driven rather than hard-coded. Decisions about how to process data are part of the knowledge of the system. In other words, a knowledge system writes its own program [Negoita, 1985].

Further more a full-scale knowledge system in the existing state should be able to exhibit the following characteristics [Hayes-Roth, 1983; Waterman, 1986; Walker, 1987]:

-- Integrate new knowledge incrementally into the knowledge system.
-- Help the designer to elicit, organize, and transfer knowledge.
-- Display knowledge in a form that is easy for people to read by having a readable and natural interface.
-- Provide explanations of its advice.
-- Reason with judgmental or inexact knowledge about the nature of a task or method of doing it efficiently.
-- Reason with declarative knowledge.

Some of these characteristics may be missing in one system or another, but they can still serve as criteria that measure the sophistication of a knowledge system.

2.2.2 Organizational Requirements for Knowledge Systems

Knowledge systems address problems which have previously been avoided because they were considered too complex. These problems have some of the following characteristics [Brown, 1984]:

-- The problem requires more than routine data manipulation (such as sorting, formatting, displaying, summarizing, etc).
-- The problem is knowledge-intensive instead of labour-intensive and hence requires dealing with the 'meaning' of data.
-- The problem is unstructured, not understood well enough to enable a straightforward procedure to be written for solving it, and deals with uncertain data.

Even though knowledge system techniques have been in existence for some time, only recently have organizations shown interest in such systems. This interest is not entirely due to the technical capability of such systems, but rather it is dependent on the organizational needs for using this advanced technology. Due to the highly competitive environment, organizational tasks have become rather complex, and this has created situations where organizations feel the need to incorporate knowledge systems in their information processing environment. Some of these situations are [Silverman, 1987; Martin & Oxman, 1988]:

-- Shortage of human expertise in key areas and the need to retain this expertise.
-- Desire to develop cost-effective business strategies and products for competing effectively.
-- Need for expertise where it is not feasible to have a human expert.
-- Need to develop more user-friendly and less complex systems.
-- Desire to allow experts to return to more important tasks and still be able to maintain the routine business activities.

Knowledge systems in their existing state are far from exhibiting human-like intelligent behaviour. Knowledge systems are currently perceived more as a sophisticated tool to aid decision making by human beings.

2.2.3 Conceptual Primitives of Knowledge Systems

The dawn of knowledge systems began with the automatic theorem proving program--the logic theorist [Newell, Shaw & Simon, 1957]. The logic theorist proved theorems in elementary logic using the notation and axioms provided by Russell and Whitehead's 'Principia' [Whitehead & Russell, 1950]. This was followed by the General Problem Solver (GPS) program [Newell & Simon, 1963]. The GPS solved problems formulated as a start state and a goal state; legal problem-solving steps were a set of operations for modifying these state representations. The GPS searched for a sequence of operations that would transform the start state into the goal state. It used 'means-ends analysis', a general control strategy for selecting among alternative state transformation operations, to guide search through the problem-space. Means-ends analysis examines the syntactic differences between the current state and the goal state and selects an operator that reduces these differences. The experimental success of GPS also started the evolution of inference control or problem solving strategies for knowledge systems.

The development of GPS was followed by other knowledge systems like MYCIN [Shortliffe, 1976] and DENDRAL [Lindsay, 1980]. These and other knowledge systems relied on the general problem solving strategies (called weak methods), but:

(i) incorporated huge knowledge bases involving large amounts of knowledge about the problem domain.
(ii) utilized a pattern-directed inference strategy [Waterman & Hayes-Roth, 1978] for inferencing from the knowledge bases.

It was felt that the availability of huge amounts of problem specific knowledge compensated for the use of weak methods in achieving solutions. Also, the pattern-directed inference mechanism provided an efficient method for searching the knowledge in the knowledge base.

The success of systems like MYCIN and DENDRAL brought about the crystallization of the conceptual components or conceptual primitives of knowledge systems. These components were based on the separation of the problem specific knowledge from the inferencing/control aspects of the knowledge system viz. Knowledge base and inference engine. The inferencing mechanism were general-purpose in nature (weak methods), again with the assumption that the strong and large knowledge contents of the knowledge base would still make the knowledge system effective. Also by having the knowledge base separate, it was easier to modify knowledge. This is succinctly specified by Edward Feigenbaum when he says:

> "The first principle of knowledge engineering is that the problem solving power exhibited by an intelligent agent's performance is primarily the consequence of its knowledge base, and only secondarily a consequence of the inference method employed. Expert systems must be knowledge-rich even if they are methods-poor. This is an important result and one that has only recently become well understood in AI. For a long time AI has focused its attentions almost exclusively on the development of clever inference methods; almost any inference method will do. The power resides in the knowledge."

The two conceptual primitives of inference engine and knowledge base organization (knowledge acquisition and representation) are now discussed.

2.2.4 Inference Engine Strategies

GPS was developed as a problem solver for some real world problems due to its symbolic manipulation of logical expressions or syntactic form of state descriptors. It was felt that by examining only the syntactic form of Sates, the GPS would indeed prove to be a 'general architecture' for intelligent problem solving, no matter what the domain. But it was soon realized that a general problem solving strategy could not solve complex problems, and so GPS was termed a 'weak problem solver', and these general problem solving strategies were termed weak methods.

Since GPS, a number of other general problem solving strategies or weak search/control strategies have emerged. These strategies provide the inference capabilities of the knowledge system. Some of the common strategies include [Rich, 1983; Luger & Stubblefield, 1989; Firebaugh, 1988]:

2.2.4.1. Generate-and-Test

Generate-and-test is a depth-first search procedure, which initially generates a possible solution by just traversing on single successive states. If the solution is not the goal state, it goes on to generate the next solution.

2.2.4.2. Hill Climbing

Hill climbing is a variant of generate-and-test in which feedback from the test procedure is used to help the generator decide which direction to move in within the search space. A heuristic function is used to decide the search direction.

2.2.4.3. Breadth-First Search

Breadth-first search in contrast to the depth-first search of generate-and-test and hill climbing, examines all the successive states that are possible from a given state. This process continues till the goal state has been reached.

2.2.4.4. Best-First Search

Best-first search is a way of combining the advantages of both depth-first and breadth-first search into a single method. So at each step, the most promising state is selected by the application of some heuristic function.

These strategies could be generally used in two ways:

1. Forward Chaining

Forward chaining (also referred to as the data-driven search), enables the problem solver to begin with the given facts of the problem. These facts when applied with some defined operations, produce new facts, which are in turn used similarly to generate more new facts. This process continues till the goal condition is achieved.

2. Backward Chaining

Backward chaining (also referred to as the goal-driven search), enables the problem solver to begin with the goal and find the operations/ conditions necessary to satisfy such a goal. These conditions in turn now become the subgoals for the search. This process continues till the actual facts are found, whence the original goal is validated.

In contrast to the weak methods, strong methods for problem-solving were suggested [Rich, 1983; Luger & Stubblefield, 1989]. These strong methods basically implied strategies which were dependent upon the knowledge of a particular problem domain. For example, a strategy for solving auto problems may be different from the strategy for solving medical problems.

2.2.5 Knowledge Representation and Acquisition

As knowledge systems began developing huge knowledge bases another issue came to the fore. This was the ability to acquire knowledge which it was now felt would provide the requisite intelligence. Acquisition of all aspects of human knowledge was becoming difficult and has since remained a major bottleneck [Hayes-Roth, 1984; Olson, 1986; Ngwenyama, 1987; Klein, Lander & Ngwenyama, 1989].

Along with knowledge acquisition came the issue of knowledge representation--how should the knowledge be represented for computer manipulation, such that it reflects intelligent behaviour. Consequently different knowledge representation schemes have come into existence, [Feigenbaum & Barr, 1981; Rich, 1983; Kobsa, 1984; Charniak & McDermott, 1987; Firebaugh, 1988; Luger & Stubblefield, 1989] viz.

-- predicate logic
-- semantic networks
-- frames
-- conceptual dependency
-- scripts
-- production rules.

Some knowledge representation schemes (like predicate logic) are more general than other schemes (like scripts). Use of a particular knowledge representation scheme depends on the type of problem-domain knowledge that needs to be stored in the knowledge base.

Much of the knowledge in knowledge systems consists of "heuristics"-rules of thumb or simplifications that effectively limit the search for solutions. Knowledge systems use heuristics because the tasks these systems undertake are typically difficult and poorly understood. They tend to resist rigorous mathematical analysis or algorithmic solutions. An algorithmic method guarantees to produce the correct or optimal solution to a problem, while a heuristic method produces an acceptable solution most of the time [Waterman, 1986]. The use of heuristic rules makes the search for solutions much easier and more practical.

Knowledge systems are in general significant improvement over conventional information systems. Knowledge systems offer a new way of designing systems that conforms more closely with the workings of the organization.

2.3 NEURAL NETWORK SYSTEMS

Knowledge systems are aimed at basically representing human intelligence. A very different approach seeks to build intelligent systems using models that emulate the structure of neurons in the human brain. Such systems are referred to as neural network systems. The exact mode and structure of such systems on the computer is still an on-going research issue and may take some time to bear fruit. But, it is increasingly felt by many in the research community that future information processing will be done on neural network systems.

2.3.1 Structure of Neurons and Neural Systems

A simple biological structure of the neural network comprises of a multitude of neurons. A neuron consists of a cell body that has a number of branched protrusions, called 'dendrites', and a single branch called the 'axon'. Dendrites receive signals from other neurons. When these combined impulses exceed a certain threshold, the neuron fires and an impulse, or ''spike'', passes down the axon. Branches at the end of the axon form 'synapses' with the dendrites of other neurons. The synapse is the point of contact between neurons; synapses may be either 'excitatory' or 'inhibitory'. An excitatory synapse adds to the total number of signals reaching the neuron; an inhibitory synapse subtracts from this total.

The above simplistic structure captures the features relevant to a neural model of computation. In particular, each computational unit is a simple thresholding device that receives signals from other units and passes a signal on to other units when its threshold is exceeded. Instead of using explicit symbols and operations, the knowledge of the system emerges out of the entire network of neural connections and threshold values.

There are a number of reasons why neural systems are appealing as mechanisms for implementing intelligence [Luger & Stubblefield, 1989]. Traditional artificial intelligence systems tend to be brittle and overly sensitive to noise; rather than degrading gracefully, such systems tend to be either right or fail completely. Human intelligence is much more flexible. Neural systems because they capture knowledge in a large number of fine-grained units, seem to have more potential for partially matching noisy and incomplete data. Also, neural systems appear to be more robust because knowledge is distributed somewhat uniformly around the network. Finally, neural systems provide a natural model for parallelism, since each neuron is an independent unit.

2.3.2 Evolution of Neural Systems

The earliest instance of a neurally based model of computation was in the work done by McCulloch and Pitts in the early 1940s [McCulloch & Pitts, 1943]. An extremely simple model of neurons was implemented that demonstrated that the power of such systems was equivalent to that of Turing machines. In the 1950s Rosenblatt proposed a neural network system that included adjustable thresholds on individual units and developed a procedure under which these networks could learn by systematically adjusting their weights [Rosenblatt, 1962]. These networks were called 'perceptrons' and were capable of learning simple classification problems.

Perceptrons were successful and widely studied. But due to their limitations (for instance their inability to recognize certain types of patterns), interest declined in them [Minsky & Papert, 1969]. Despite their limitations however, perceptrons laid much of the foundation for the modern work on neural systems.

Modern work in neural systems began in the 1980s under the name of 'connectionism'. The approaches include Hopfield nets [Hopfield, 1982], Boltzmann machines [Hinton and Sejnowski, 1986], and multilayer networks with back propagation [Rumelhart *et al.*, 1986]. These approaches have overcome the limitations of perceptrons, but are still a long way from their biological counterpart.

In spite of the rapidly growing interest in neural systems as a basis for parallel computation, there is currently a need for neural structures that will allow for the development of tractable formalisms [Feldman, 1988]. Such formalisms can then serve as a basis for theoretical systems neuroscience, which can then be experimented with. If the formalisms are appropriate, they should play the conventional role of a scientific language that has been largely lacking in system-level neuroscience [Robinson, 1988].

2.4 SUMMARY OF ADVANCES AND UNRESOLVED ISSUES

Information processing systems have undergone major changes as can be seen from the above discussion. These changes have had considerable influence on the organization's structure and working. But these changes are not mutually exclusive. Information processing systems based on conventional information systems concepts dealt with two levels of intelligence:

-- know what (about UoD-data),
-- know how (about procedures).

But, the development of information processing systems based on knowledge system concepts has broadened the horizon with the inclusion of two additional levels of intelligence:

-- know why (reflective thinking),
-- know that (fundamental assumptions).

This broadening of the intelligence horizon which provides a continuum in the development of information processing systems, also is a reflection of the conceptual advance made by information processing systems. But, along with the conceptual advance, information processing systems have also affected the core of organizational design and development. This impact on organization development reflects the organizational advance made by information processing systems. A brief discussion of the organizational impact now follows.

2.4.1 Impact on Organizations

Development and usage of information processing systems is closely linked with the way organizations are designed. Organizational design is the search for a coherence or a fit among goals and purposes for which an organization exists with how the organization should be structured, as well as the integration of individuals with the specified structure and its goals and purposes [Clark, 1972; Galbraith, 1977; Hanna, 1988]. Information processing systems can also be perceived as providing a coherence or fit among organizations strategy, structure and individuals. A general organizational design theory cannot be applicable to all organizations completely, but only partially with the remaining aspects of design issues varying and depending upon an organization's uniqueness. Similarly the information processing systems of one organization cannot be mapped in their entirety from one organization to another, although they can partially. Such systems will vary among organizations depending upon each organization's design considerations.

Due to the close proximity between organization design and information processing systems, a perspective on the advancement in information processing systems can be properly ascertained by viewing the impact of such systems on key organization design variables. Now organization designs are largely influenced by the application of various management theories. Each such theory, viz. classical/structural theory [Weber, 1947; Parsons, 1960]; human relations theory [Mayo, 1945]; managerial/scientific management theory [Taylor, 1911; Fayol, 1950]; technology theory [March & Simon, 1958; Thompson, 1967] and institutional theory [Perrow, 1970], provides an approach to designing organizations so as to optimize their existence. Also each such theory provides some key variables which are considered crucial for the organization's success. The emphasis is on integrating these various approaches to determine the variables necessary for optimal organizational design. These design variables have been identified as [Galbraith, 1977; Hanna, 1988] strategy, structure, tasks, individuals, reward system, information and decision-making. Table 2.1 shows a matrix of the impact various information processing systems (briefly outlined in section 2.1.1 along with knowledge systems) have had on these design variables. The impact shown in the table is a preliminary attempt to indicate the advancements such systems have brought in the perception and usage of 'information' in the organization. The table illustrates a viewpoint and is interpretative.

However in spite of the continued growth information processing system development and its impact on organizations, there still exist some major drawbacks. A summary of advances and drawbacks is discussed below for each of the three types of information processing system. These drawbacks also reflect on the shortcomings of the conceptual primitives utilized for system development.

2.4.2 Advances and Limitations of Information Systems

The evolution of information systems from processing of routine and structured information (e.g. transaction processing systems) to the processing of non-routine and semi-structured information (e.g. decision support systems and executive support systems) is of immense significance. The handling of semi-structured information enables the information system to be used for strategic decision-making. This has consequently brought a change in the perception of information systems

TABLE 2.1: Information Processing Systems Impact on Organizational Design Variables

Organization Design Variables	Information Processing System Types					
	TPS	MIS	DSS	ESS	OAS	KS
Strategy				Y	Y	Y
Tasks	Y	Y	Y		Y	Y
Structure			Y	Y		Y
Individual			Y			Y
Reward System		Y				
Information & Decision		Y	Y	Y	Y	Y

within the organization.

Information systems have by virtue of improved tools and computer technology provided the organization with better products and services. This has focused attention on the strategic value and nature of "information". Organizations now perceive the tapping and the effective utilization of information as important for the ultimate success of their organization. In fact successful organizations do not perceive the attainment of their goals and objectives without the proper harnessing of their "information" resource. These advances in the perception and utilization of information systems have been largely due to the way the two distinct concepts of 'data' and 'procedures' have evolved. The full utilization of database theory has improved the handling and storing of data, while the fourth generation languages have brought a much wider participation and usage of information systems.

In spite of the tremendous advances made in the evolution of information systems some fundamental issues still remain unresolved. Some of these are [Tsichritzis & Lochovsky, 1982; Laudon & Laudon, 1988]:

1. Much of the essential information in an organization is inherently unstructured and therefore cannot be captured and represented by structured techniques. Consequently views and perspectives contrary to organizational defined rules are not included. This reduces the scope of the information generated by the information systems. So it is important to either include

these perspectives or to have information structures dealing with these perspectives specified.

2. The value of information depends on its analysis, interpretation, explanation and finally understanding by the user. Information requires a context. This context is supplied by the user's stock or core of knowledge. Unless this context is provided the value of information provided by the information system is low, which should not be so.
3. Incorporation of the time factor in the information represented and generated by the system.

2.4.3 Advances and Limitations of Knowledge Systems

Knowledge systems were concerned with the development of systems that represented intelligent behaviour. Hence they were provided capabilities that could not be easily represented in conventional information systems. Many researchers have hypothesized the need of having knowledge-based information systems [Bubenko, 1983; Crawford, 1984; Bubenko, 1986; Sibley, 1986; Berztiss, 1986; Carlson, 1988; Belkin *et al.,* 1987]. Conventionally, information processing systems based on knowledge systems concepts were characterized as automated decision support systems or part of the tools of a decision support system [Sprague & McNurlin, 1988; Laudon & Laudon, 1988; Fox, 1983]. This narrow view has unfairly reduced the promise inherent in such systems for broader applications.

There are many fundamental issues that are unresolved in knowledge systems. Some of these are [Waterman, 1986; Martin & Oxman, 1988]:

1. New mechanisms for knowledge representation (knowledge structures) are needed so that much broader contexts and types of human knowledge can be represented. This may go a long way to easing the knowledge acquisition bottleneck.
2. Inferencing capabilities are weak in knowledge systems. There is an urgent need for general purpose inferencing techniques (that may also incorporate some 'learning' capabilities), to improve systems intelligence and reasoning.
3. It is felt that by using production rules there is a natural modularity in knowledge bases. But as knowledge base increases in size, this modularity turns into complexity. It is important that new approaches to modularity be developed, which will

not dissolve as the knowledge base expands.

4. Technical issues of integrity and consistency of knowledge when there are concurrent users have yet to be resolved.
5. Organizational issues reflecting the impact of knowledge systems still remain unresolved, such as impact of knowledge systems on organizational and individual performance, factors responsible for knowledge system acceptance, and so on.

2.4.4 Limitations of Neural Network Systems

Neural network systems fundamentally offer a new approach to information processing. Although these systems have still not reached a commercial/workable level, the various unresolved issues relate to their research claims. Some of these are:

1. The human brain is felt to be a highly structured and organized system. Knowledge of such a system is still not complete. More needs to be done on this, if neural networks are to be effective.
2. The human brain also has other mechanisms for learning and expanding its neural network. These aspects are not accounted for in existing research.
3. All human activities are not parallel. Much higher-level reasoning and problem-solving behaviour seems to be quite serial in nature. In these cases neural network systems should also provide serial processing capabilities.

3

REVIEW OF INFORMATION PROCESSING CONCEPTUAL ARCHITECTURES

The term "conceptual architecture" has been used in various contexts in the area of information processing. My view of conceptual architecture here is concerned with the way in which the primitive concepts involved in the building of information processing systems are integrated to make such systems operable. Since the beginning of information processing system development various conceptual architectures have evolved. The evolution of these conceptual architectures has been primarily due to a combination of changing organizational requirements and technology improvements.

In this chapter the evolution of conceptual architectures in information processing systems and their structure/framework is described. At the end of the chapter the limitations of the architectures for the open-system approach are outlined. Since neural network systems are still in the research and conceptualization stage, their architectural trends (if they can be said to exist at all) are not considered.

Prior to the emergence and use of knowledge systems in organizations, all information system architectures evolved around the concept of data (data-based architectures). Now due to the prevalence of knowledge system concepts, architectures supporting such knowledge-based information systems, also called intelligent information systems (IIS), are evolving. This survey of conceptual architectures will provide a perspective on existing architectures along with their limitations, thereby pointing to the need for the formulation of the open intelligent information system (OIIS) architecture in the next chapter.

3.1 DATA-BASED ARCHITECTURES

Data-based architectures have been the traditional mode on which information processing systems (information systems) have been built. The evolution of these architectures has thus been synonymous with the evolution of information systems. There have been three such types of architectures for information systems development:

1. File-centered architectures.
2. Database-centered architectures.
3. Distributed database-centered architectures.

3.1.1 File-Centered Architectures

The major role of information systems in the early stages (1960's) was to perform well defined (and limited) clerical tasks such as inventory and payroll. The basic organizational requirement and thrust was for streamlining routine departmental operations so as to reduce cost and improve the efficiency of such operations. Systems tended to be built opportunistically, and not according to some grand plan. Each functional area developed systems in isolation from other functional areas. The degree of integration, if any, was low. Systems were built to last for many years. This was necessary due to the considerable investment required to achieve an operational system. Also, most of the systems were not embedded within the organization, i.e. their operation was not time-critical to the organization.

The dominant architecture in these early stages was the file-centered architecture-interaction of the application programs (containing procedures) with files (containing data), as shown in Figure 3.1. In Figure 3.1 it is assumed that one application may interact with one or more files, and simultaneously a file may also be accessed by more than one application. Also each application can have its own separate set of files. It was felt that applications needed exclusive files for each department of functional areas pre-specified and unique procedures.

File-centered architectures were used predominantly for some routine processing of transactions and standard reports, and as such their impact on organization's overall performance and effectiveness was reduced.

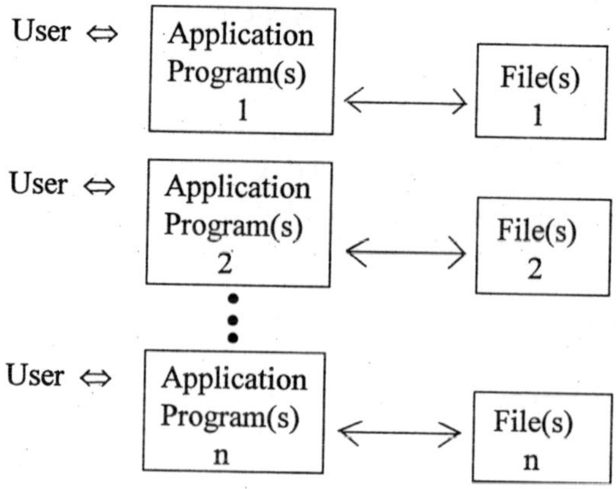

FIG. 3.1

3.1.2 Database-Centered Architectures

The 1970s view of the architecture of an information system was dominated by the database. After the success of file-centered information processing systems in various functional areas, the organizational needs now focused on using systems for more general organizational activities like planning and scheduling. Since these new systems needed data from different functional areas (each having separate file-centered systems), the need was felt for integrating data existing in these separate functional areas. Due to the severe limitations of the file-centered architecture, the newly emergent database concepts and technology were considered necessary to overcome the drawbacks in existing systems.

Essentially information processing systems now comprised of application databases and few files as shown in Figure 3.2. The need for having data files along with a database (Figure 3.2) arose because information system developers were basically integrating the newly arrived database concepts/systems with the existing application files. For operational reasons, much of the data was still maintained in data files. But, again such an architecture only brought proliferation of databases, as each application had a separate database.

Naturally, as the advantages of database operations could not be achieved by having this mix of databases and files, redundancy and inconsistency of data grew. Although database technology had permeated the systems design phase, its use was incorrect and the impact of systems based on this architecture on organizational performance and effectiveness was again limited. Nevertheless this limited usage of the database also brought the dawn of the database-centered architecture, which has since evolved until now.

The changing role of the information system from performing numerical and well defined clerical tasks to a more general information utility brought further modifications in the database-centered architecture. As systems began operating in real-time environments, and got 'embedded' in the workings of the organization, they started affecting

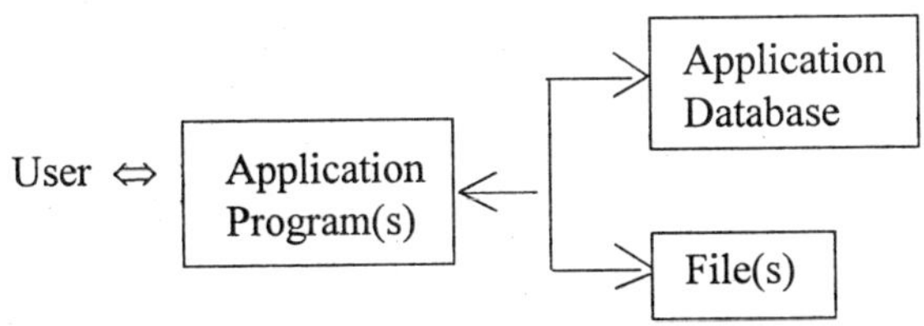

FIG. 3.2

organizational productivity and efficiency, individual and group decision-making and the organization's strategic goals. However the need was felt to come out of the mode of capturing data on the basis of application or functional areas. The stress shifted to planning the storage and usage of organization-wide data so that information could be efficiently harnessed. Consequently two variations of the database-centered architecture evolved which are now discussed [Martin, 1983; Lee, 1984].

One such variation was the concept of having subject databases. Databases were largely independent of the specific application. Now application programs interacted with more than one database at a time, depending on the breadth of the subject/function areas the application was catering to, as shown in Figure 3.3. This led to faster application development, but if not managed well it tended to disintegrate into a file-centered environment with the same data stored in different databases.

This architecture (Figure 3.3) allowed the building of better and more efficient systems. Consequently the impact of this architecture on organizational design and philosophy was greater. Systems built on this architecture could now be utilized for improving organizational productivity and performance much more effectively.

The other variation originated when, instead of different subject databases, a single database for the entire organization was developed, with which all users (analysts, end-users, etc.) interacted, as shown in

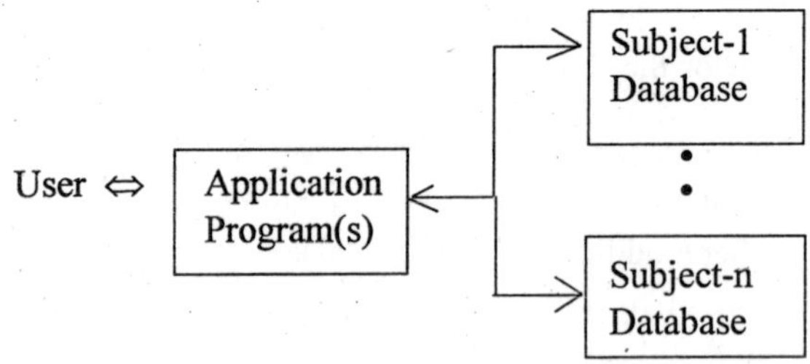

FIG. 3.3

Figure 3.4. This obviously is the architecture that is currently in vogue. The introduction of fourth generation languages has also augmented this view by query language facilities, form definition and processing facilities, report generators, dictionaries, graphics packages, spreadsheets, and so on. The heart of the system built around such facilities is normally a relational database (or a database-centered architecture).

The architecture based on single database (Figure 3.4) provided full capability to effectively nurture information as a resource. Consequently its impact on organizational productivity and performance was tremendous.

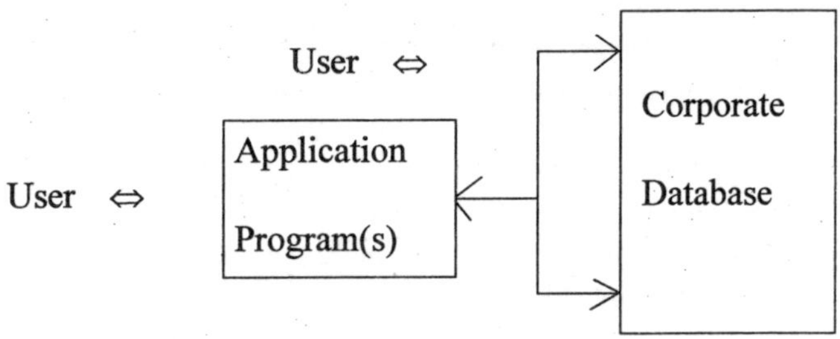

FIG. 3.4

3.1.3 Distributed Database-Centered Architectures

Distributed database-centered architectures were an extension of the database-centered architectural philosophy. The need for distributed information system development which led to the development of such architectures was primarily due to the changing nature of the business environment and the advancement in computer technology, as well as the successful use of centralized database architectures in improving organizational performance [Buchanan & Linowes, 1980; Sprague & McNurlin, 1986; Kroenke & Dolan, 1988].

Distributed database architectures provided the capability for integrating information processing in a geographically dispersed environment, thereby further improving organizational performance. There were certain organizational exigencies that created the need to incorporate distributed database architectures in the organization. Some of the requirements that forced the need for distributing data are [Martin, 1982; Sprague & McNurlin, 1986]:

1. Data are normally used at a particular location, but rarely or never used at other locations.
2. The accuracy, privacy, and security of the data are a local responsibility.
3. Local users have more knowledge of procedures and quality of data than users at any other location.
4. The access/update rate is too high to store relevant data at a remote location.

Information processing systems based on distributed database architectures provide for the development of databases at separate locations (called nodes) and then integrate the processing at these individual nodes into an overall framework. In other words, these architectures consist of many individual nodes which are separate information processing entities with their own databases, which are integrated in a framework (conceptual architecture) for the working of the entire information processing system.

Distributed database architectures have evolved in two directions:

1. Logically centralized but physically decentralized databases called composite database architectures.
2. Logically decentralized and physically decentralized databases called federated database architectures.

Both of these architectures are now discussed.

3.1.3.1 Composite Database Architectures

The composite database architecture is the conventional architecture for distributed information systems [Lien & Ying, 1978; Rothnie *et al.*,

1980; Litwin, 1980; Litwin, 1981; Ceri & Pelagatti, 1984]. In such an architecture there exists a single conceptual schema for the entire information system. Users and applications at different nodes access the data stored in their local databases, which however is monitored by a

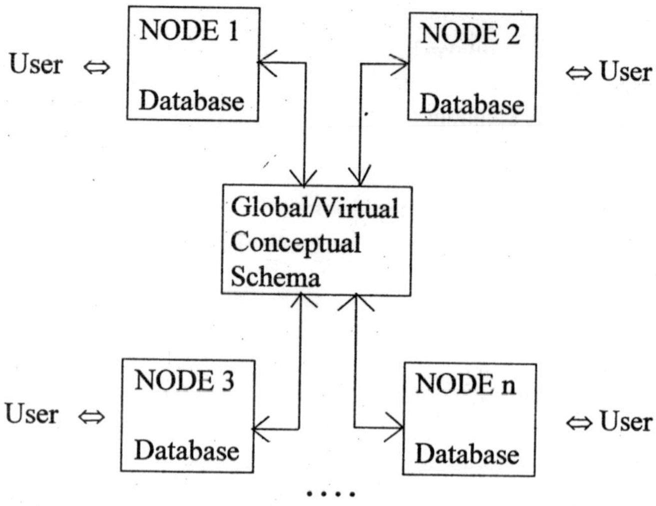

FIG. 3.5

single global/virtual conceptual schema as shown in Figure 3.5.

There are many existing database systems like R* [Lindsay & Selinger, 1980], Multibase [Smith *et al.,* 1981] and Superviews [Motro & Buneman, 1981], which reflect this composite database architecture.

The composite database architecture is the logical extension of the centralized database architecture (Figure 3.4) discussed earlier. This point of view is evident when access by any user at a particular node to a data item at another node is first kept relatively uniform by virtue of corresponding to a logically centralized global schema and then the access is channeled through a centralized entity. So the overall database consistency, integrity and control becomes the responsibility of the centralized entity. However it is possible to have some local authority at the individual node database, but the ultimate responsibility is with the administrator entrusted with the development and maintenance of the global/virtual schema.

3.1.3.2 Federated Database Architectures

The federated database architecture which is also referred to as the Decentralized Autonomous Cooperating Information System (DACIS) architecture is a very recent idea [Hammer & McLeod, 1980; Heimbigner & McLeod, 1981; Heimbigner, 1982; Heimbigner & McLeod, 1985; Heimbigner, 1987; Johannesson & Wangler, 1989]. This architecture allows the development of autonomous databases for each individual node. The different nodes then cooperate in order to communicate data and meta data (knowledge about what information is available) by explicit interfaces.

In an information system based on the federated database architecture no single database at a node has authority over another database at some other node as there is no global schema for the overall information system. Each node must control its interaction with other nodes itself and decide what information to import and export by virtue of negotiation. Each node gradually builds its own local view of the total database by integrating the information of its local schema with the information it imports from other nodes.

In order for any node to know about the existence of another node in the information system, a federal dictionary is utilized which contains names and addresses of all participating nodes in the system, as shown in Figure 3.6.

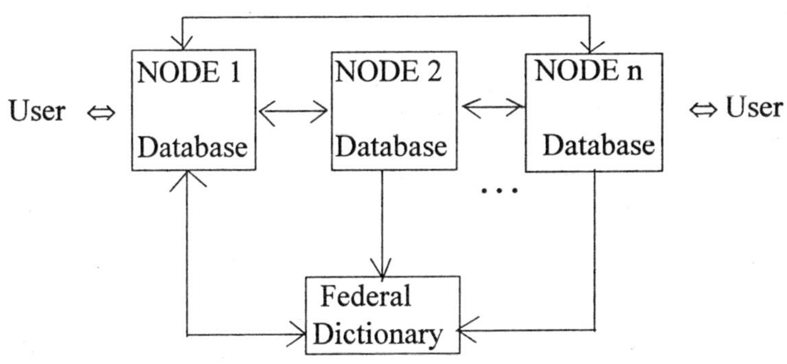

FIG. 3.6

The local database structure at each node in this architecture consists of three parts:

1. The private or local schema, which contain data that is local to

the node's requirements.

2. The export schema, which consist of data that the node is willing to share with other nodes in the system.
3. The import schema, which specify the data the node desires to use from other nodes in the system.

Now in order to import information, each node must know or discover what information is available in the system. This is accomplished in two steps. First, through the federal dictionary each node may discover the names and network addresses of the other nodes in the system. Second, each node contacts those nodes, using a predefined protocol. At this point a node is in a position to peruse the export schema of the other nodes and engage in the schema importation process. When a node has imported information, it must then integrate that information with its own local schema.

Further research is under way to utilize the federated database architecture in information system development [Clemm *et al.*, 1985; Johannesson, 1988].

3.2 KNOWLEDGE-BASED ARCHITECTURES

Knowledge-based architectures provide the basis for developing knowledge-based information systems, referred to as Intelligent Information Systems (IIS). IIS, as mentioned earlier, are built for those applications where 'knowledge' can be expressed in a formal language and where the system is supposed to maintain, acquire and process knowledge in a formal way. There have been two types of intelligent information system architectures:

1. Production systems.
2. Blackboard systems.

3.2.1 Production Systems

Production systems have been the initial architecture for knowledge-based system development [Newell & Simon, 1972], and then have been the basis for such pioneering intelligent systems as DENDRAL [Lindsay, 1980] and MYCIN [Shortliffe, 1976]. Intelligent systems based on this architecture typically have the following components (as shown in Figure 3.7):

1. Knowledge base.
2. Inference engine.
3. User interface.

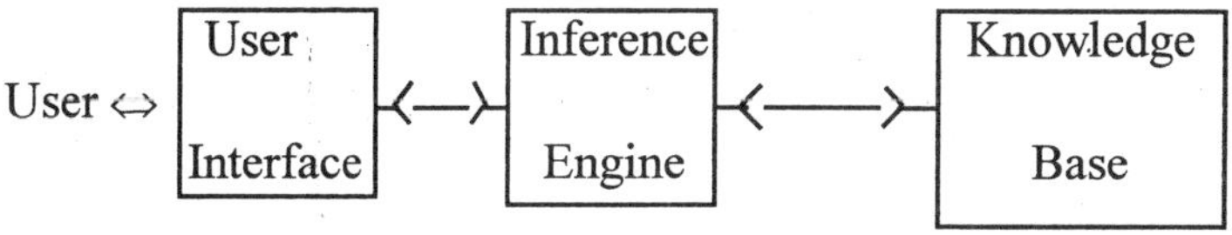

FIG. 3.7

Each of these components is now described. This description provides as outline of the way intelligent systems could be utilized in organizations [Bubenko, 1983].

3.2.1.1 Knowledge Base Structure

The knowledge base in general contains the syntax of the formal language to be used when communicating with the system. The syntax will (1) define what kind of assertions can be made and understood about the application; and (2) include descriptions of the semantics of the concepts used in the formal language for describing phenomena, relationships, etc. of the UoD of the application. Using first order logic, the syntax part is dealt with by predicate symbols and their meaning.

One part of the knowledge base is the "rule part", which will contain a set of formal definitions of assumptions made and rules established concerning the structure and behaviour of the application UoD. These rules tell what assertions about the UoD are valid (or reasonable) and how certain assertions are related to (or can be derived from) other assertions. They must also include knowledge about transactions and operations on applications--the 'statics' and 'dynamics' of the application. Again using first order logic, the "rule part" would comprise a set of closed well-formed formulas concerning the application UoD.

The other part of the knowledge base consists of a set of facts observed in, or asserted as true about the UoD. Conceptually, it also contains the facts that can be derived from the observed or asserted facts and the rules in the 'rule' part of the knowledge base. Using first order logic, the 'fact' part contains a set of ground instances concerning the application UoD.

Thus, according to the first order logic framework, the syntax and the rule part can now be seen as a theory about the application and the fact part as an interpretation of it. This enables the intelligent systems to build such knowledge bases more methodically by 'self describing' not only the data or facts (as is done in the data dictionary), but also the 'logic' behind the processing of the facts.

3.2.1.2 Inference Engine Structure

The inference engine called the 'reasoning' processor contains an "interpreter" that decides how to apply the rules to infer new knowledge and a "scheduler" that decides the order in which the rules should be applied. It thus consists of problem independent inference control strategies which determine which knowledge rule should be executed next and executes the action specified. In other words, the inference engine decides how to add/modify previous beliefs in solving problems depending on the various problem-solving strategies.

3.2.1.3 User Interface

The user-interface is the development of a user-friendly front end, which according to Michie [Michie, 1982] serves as a cognitive window for the user. The user-interface manages the human-machine dialogue during the problem solving process.

An extension of this architecture called 'structured production systems' [Pau, 1986] has been proposed. This architecture divides the knowledge base into knowledge chunks and uses meta-rules to determine which knowledge chunk should be accessed next.

In spite of its major deficiency of having the provision of a single monolithic knowledge base in its framework, which might degrade performance with increasing knowledge base size, it is still the preferred architecture for intelligent information systems [Nilsson, 1980; Hayes-Roth, 1983; Rich, 1983; Kulikowski & Weiss, 1984; Harmon & King, 1985; Charniak & McDermott, 1987; Firebaugh, 1988; Floyd, 1988].

3.2.2 Blackboard Systems

Due to the complexity of knowledge in the knowledge base, especially when it pertains to different areas of expertise in an organization and its unmaintainability due to increase in knowledge base size, it is necessary to devise mechanisms by which intelligent information systems could be made modular and structured. Incorporating modularity in intelligent systems is not straightforward and is different from conventional information systems. So unlike the conventional information systems where modularity is achieved by having techniques of modular procedure specifications (with a monolithic corporate database), an intelligent system (which now has standardized inference mechanisms) has to achieve modularity in the knowledge of the knowledge base.

The thrust consequently has been to have multiple knowledge bases and then distribute the knowledge to different knowledge bases of the intelligent system. Intelligent systems are then expected to generate solutions to problems by making such distributed knowledge bases "cooperate". Problem solving now becomes cooperative in that sharing of knowledge becomes necessary to allow the system as a whole to produce solutions [Huhns, 1987; Durfee & Lesser & Corkill, 1987]. This thinking generated a new discipline in artificial intelligence, called distributed artificial intelligence or distributed problem solving. The premises made and approaches taken by distributed problem solving are now discussed.

3.2.2.1 Distributed Problem Solving Characteristics

Distributed problem solving consists of multiple knowledge bases/ knowledge systems which "cooperate" by communicating with each other for problem solving [Smith, 1985; Durfee & Lesser & Corkill, 1985; Gasser, 1987; Sridharan, 1987; Corkill & Lesser, 1987; Gasser & Braganza & Herman, 1987]. Two principal forms of cooperation have evolved [Smith & Davis, 1981; Davis & Smith, 1983]:

1. Task-sharing.
2. Result-sharing.

Both of these forms of cooperation are now discussed.

In the task-sharing approach the problem/task is decomposed into a number of subproblems. Each subproblem is an autonomous knowledge system (node) and so the effects of the individual node's actions are primarily local. Problem decomposition is through explicit task-subtask connections. The resulting hierarchy becomes useful as a means of structuring answer synthesis. To solve the overall problem the various nodes exchange knowledge that may be necessary to find a solution. A communication protocol [Smith, 1980] is provided whereby the various nodes can enter into negotiation and be coordinated for problem solving. The task-sharing approach is most useful for problem domains in which it is appropriate to define a hierarchy of subtasks or levels of abstraction (eg. audio or video signal interpretation).

In the result-sharing approach, the problem/task is decomposed again into a number of subproblems (autonomous knowledge systems). But unlike the task-sharing approach where the communication pattern is explicit, here the different autonomous knowledge systems compute partial results on the basis of the limited knowledge available to them. These results are then communicated to the other autonomous knowledge systems (nodes). Results received from the nodes form the basis for further refinements. An iterative process (where the intermediate steps for each node include communicating partial results, refining the knowledge set, computing new results, combining old ideas, and generating new ones) leads to a solution of the given problem. Result-sharing is useful in problem domains where results achieved by one individual node influence other nodes and this sharing of results enables convergence to a solution.

To achieve the development of intelligent information systems having distributed problem solving capability, conceptual architectures were needed that provided a framework for the various autonomous nodes to cooperate for problem solving. One such major existing conceptual architecture for distributed problem solving is called the "blackboard systems" [Jagannathan & Dodhiawala, 1987], which is now described.

3.2.2.2 Blackboard Architecture Components

The blackboard architecture was first developed in the context of the HEARSAY-II speech understanding project [Erman, 1980]. The idea behind the blackboard approach is simple. The entire system consists of a set of independent modules, called knowledge sources (or knowledge systems), that contain the domain-specific knowledge in the system, and a blackboard--a shared data structure, to which all the knowledge systems have access. Each module can have its own knowledge representation scheme as shown in Figure 3.8. The knowledge sources respond opportunistically to changes in the blackboard. In other words, pieces of knowledge are applied either backwards or forwards at the most "opportune" time [Nii, 1986].

The hypotheses on the blackboard are arranged along two dimensions: level (from small, low-level hypotheses about individual sounds to large, high-level hypotheses about the meaning of an entire sentence) and time (corresponding to time periods of the utterance being analyzed). The goal of the system is to create a single hypothesis that represents a solution to the problem.

When a knowledge system is activated it examines the current contents of the blackboard and applies its knowledge either to create a new 'hypothesis' and write it on the blackboard, or to modify an existing one. Although the execution of the entire HEARSAY-II system consists of the asynchronous execution of a collection of knowledge systems, the execution of an individual knowledge system is a sequential process. Once a knowledge system is activated, it executes without being interrupted until it is finished.

The actual determination of which knowledge system should be activated next is done by a special knowledge system, called the 'scheduler', on the basis of its knowledge about how best to conduct the search in the particular domain. The scheduler uses ratings supplied to it by each of the independent knowledge systems. If the scheduler ever discovers that there are no activation records pending, then the system's execution terminates.

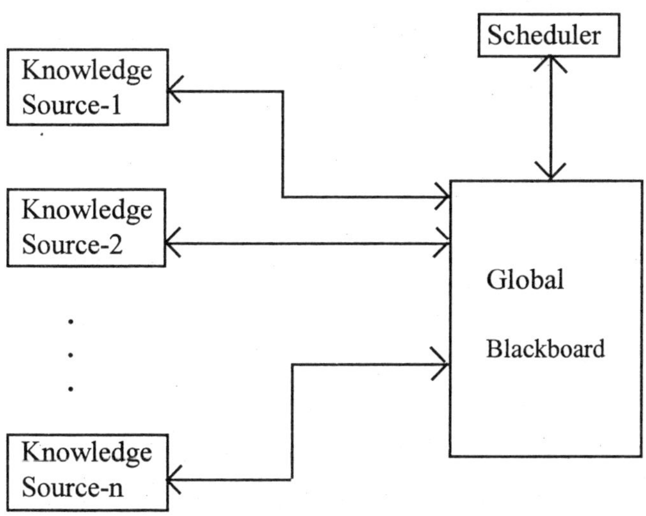

FIG. 3.8

The techniques developed in HEARSAY-II have since been generalized into HEARSAY-III [Balzer *et al.*, 1980; Erman *et al.*, 1981]. The blackboard architecture was the primary architecture that allowed distributed intelligent information systems development, and has been the basis of intelligent systems such as CODER [Fox, 1987], CRYSALIS [Terry, 1983] and TRICERO [Williams, Brown & Barnes, 1984].

3.3 LIMITATIONS OF CURRENT ARCHITECTURES

The different data-based and knowledge-based architectures have been used as the foundation of a variety of systems in organizations. However from the perspective of the open-systems approach for intelligent systems development there are certain limitations in these conceptual architectures preventing their use. This section describes these limitations.

3.3.1 Limitations of File-Centered Architectures

File-centered architectures are not adequate for the open-systems approach: they have the severe limitations for which reason they were themselves augmented by other previous architectures. Some of the major limitations of file-centered architectures are [Martin, 1983]:

1. High level of 'redundancy' as same type of data item is stored in many different files. This also naturally leads to severe 'inconsistency' in data values--different versions of the same data in different stages of update, as well as erosion of any data item's 'integrity'.
2. Inability to group existing data items differently for ad-hoc queries without major restructuring, thereby making it 'inflexible'.
3. It can be expensive to make changes to the file system itself and consequently the entire system.

3.3.2 Limitations of Database-Centered Architectures

Database-centered architectures (Section 3.1.2 and Section 3.1.3) cannot be directly used for open-architecture intelligent systems due to their non-support for knowledge bases and other knowledge system components. However the evolution of these architectures reflects the strides made in the development of conventional information systems.

The two distributed database architectures (Section 3.1.3.1 and Section 3.1.3.2) have some similarity with the notion of distributing the processing in an open-architecture system environment. However their assumptions impose certain limitations as discussed below.

In a composite database architecture, one of the main purpose of forcing each node to conform to a global schema is to guarantee consistency over the total system. But consistency in a strict sense is a practical impossibility even in centralized database systems with one global schema, and will be even more difficult to achieve in a distributed database environment with a single global/virtual schema [Lyngbaek & McLeod, 1984; Heimbigner & McLeod, 1985; Johannesson & Wangler, 1989].

Also inherent in the concept of integration in composite database architecture is the existence of some central authority responsible for designing and maintaining the databases at the various nodes. The local developers at each node who may have expended considerable resources in developing their databases may be reluctant to lose control of them. Further more changes to the structure of the database at any node must pass through the central database administrator, who when weighing similar competing demands for change from other individual nodes, will find it difficult to decide on changes to make [Hewitt & deJong, 1983; Hewitt & deJong, 1984; Heimbigner & McLeod, 1985].

Research is still continuing on improving the consistency, integrity, recovery and security in composite database architectures [Holland, 1983; Kroenke & Dolan, 1988].

The federated database architecture is most closely related to the notion of distributed problem solving and the open-system approach [Bubenko & Lindencrona, 1986; Johannesson & Wangler, 1989]. However as it is not concerned with issues involved in intelligent system development, it cannot be directly utilized in open-architecture intelligent system development.

3.3.3 Limitations of Production Systems Architecture

Developing intelligent information systems using a knowledge-based architecture provides many advantages over conventional data-based information systems. But the production systems architecture which is the basis for many of the intelligent information systems has drawbacks for distributed and open-architecture intelligent systems.

1. Since there is provision of a single knowledge base there is difficulty in distributing knowledge within this monolithic knowledge base. This leads to difficulty in managing knowledge as the knowledge base expands or whenever changes in the knowledge base are performed (like addition, deletion or modification).
2. As knowledge may span different subject areas, difficulty in managing knowledge when the knowledge base is expanding may also cause difficulty in ensuring consistency/integrity of the knowledge base.
3. Sometimes there might be a need to represent portions of knowledge in different knowledge representation schemes. In a monolithic knowledge base it might be difficult to have different knowledge representation schemes.

Due to the above mentioned major limitations with the production systems architecture, it cannot be directly used for open-architecture intelligent systems. However as open-architecture intelligent systems comprise of many small autonomous intelligent subsystems, it is possible to build these autonomous intelligent subsystems with the production systems architecture, as now the knowledge base will be small and manageable.

3.3.4 Limitations of Blackboard Systems Architecture

The blackboard systems architecture, in spite of its provision for modularity and mechanisms for achieving "cooperation" among various autonomous knowledge systems, does not consider "how" a specific piece of knowledge (hypothesis) communicated by an autonomous knowledge system should be handled by another autonomous knowledge system, i.e. the nature of communication semantics is weak. Simply posting the hypothesis on the blackboard is a very restricted form of communication when the overall purpose of the system is to imitate human thinking processes. Mode of communication semantics should be determined by the autonomous knowledge system initiating the communication and not an independent scheduler. The nature of communication semantics is important for an intelligent system based on the open-system approach.

The scheduler is also supposed to form its own judgement on hypothesis on the blackboard based on the responses given by the autonomous knowledge system. But, having the scheduler independently decide among the responses, without having any background knowledge about the hypothesis, may reduce the coherence and focus of the overall system. The scheduler orders the execution of the autonomous knowledge systems based on the ordering in which the blackboard is searched rather than considering the current state of the problem which caused an autonomous knowledge system to post the hypothesis [Corkill, 1983; Green, 1987]. This approach may work if the general abstraction levels leading to a solution can be specified before hand (as specified by the hierarchical layers of the blackboard in HEARSAY and other implementations). But it may be difficult to always predict the abstraction levels introduced during the solution of a problem--that is where the versatility of a truly intelligent system lies.

The blackboard systems architecture is the only major conceptual architecture for distributed problem-solving intelligent systems. However in order to achieve the objective of developing of open-architecture intelligent systems, avoiding the limitations of the blackboard systems architecture, it is necessary to provide a framework which allows an effective partitioning of the knowledge into different autonomous knowledge systems and provide proper communication semantics by which such autonomous knowledge sources can cooperate with each other for problem solving. In other words, there is a need to develop knowledge-based architectures following the open-systems approach for intelligent information processing systems.

4

AN OPEN INTELLIGENT INFORMATION SYSTEMS ARCHITECTURE

It is increasingly being recognized that knowledge-based architectures should be able to distribute knowledge and so provide for modularity. This will enable them to handle the complexity of the enlarged knowledge bases of organizations, thereby making intelligent systems more effective in a wider context. Due to this necessity, production systems were framed (unsuccessfully) as structured production systems so as to overcome the drawback of their monolithic knowledge base. Also the distributed problem-solving approach and its predominant conceptual architecture, the blackboard systems, provided the framework for integrating the separate knowledge sources, primarily out of this concern. However these conceptual architectures are still not compatible with the requirements of the open-systems approach to intelligent information systems.

In this chapter we first survey the major issues involved in the open-systems approach in general and then the concepts relevant to a conceptual architecture for Open Intelligent Information Systems (OIIS) are provided. The fundamentals for the creation of the OIIS architecture are outlined next. The chapter ends with a discussion of the advances made by the development of the OIIS architecture.

4.1 OPEN-SYSTEMS APPROACH CHARACTERISTICS

The promise of the open-systems approach for information processing has already been outlined earlier (Section 1.3). An attempt is made here to explain the characteristics of this approach and the major issues involved in its use as a philosophy for intelligent information systems development.

4.1.1 Properties of Open-Systems

The open-systems approach to developing intelligent systems is similar to organizational design and management. It consists of many autonomous intelligent systems that are logically interconnected for problem-solving. Open-systems have no predefined hierarchy or planning in distributing knowledge and so are always subject to communications between autonomous intelligent systems. Open-architecture intelligent systems are characterized by the following properties [Hewitt & de Jong, 1983; Hewitt & de Jong, 1984; Hewitt, 1985; Hewitt, 1986, Gerson & Star, 1986].

4.1.1.1. Continuous Change and Evolution

Autonomous intelligent systems must be able to change as the components and demands placed on them change. Moreover they must be able to evolve new internal components in order to accommodate the shifting work they perform.

4.1.1.2. Arm's-length Relationships and Decentralized Decision-making

In general the autonomous intelligent systems do not have direct access to one another's internal knowledge. Arm's length relationships imply that the open-systems framework may accommodate multiple computers at different physical sites or multiple autonomous intelligent systems that do not have access to the internal components of others. This leads to decentralized decision-making.

4.1.1.3. Perpetual Inconsistency among Knowledge Bases

Because of privacy and discretionary concerns, the knowledge bases of the autonomous intelligent systems will contain different perspectives and conflicting beliefs. Thus all the knowledge bases in the complete system will be perpetually inconsistent. Decentralization makes it impossible to update all the knowledge bases simultaneously. This implies that it is not even possible to know what kinds of knowledge are contained in all the local knowledge bases at any one time. Systems must be able to operate in the presence of inconsistent and incomplete knowledge bases.

4.1.1.4. Need for Negotiation among System Components

In a highly distributed environment, no system directly controls the resources of another. The various autonomous intelligent systems must persuade one another to cooperate in problem-solving. Consequently any open-systems framework/architecture must support a mechanism for negotiation among involved autonomous intelligent systems.

4.1.1.5. Inadequacy of the Closed-world Assumption

The closed-world assumption is that the information being modelled about the world is complete in the sense that exactly those relationships that hold among objects can be derived from the local information possessed by the system. Systems that depend on the closed-world assumptions make use of the principle that they can find all existing instances of a concept by searching their local storage (database/ knowledge base). This assumption is universal in the information processing literature. Such assumptions enable systems to provide ready default solutions for any query. Unfortunately, the default solutions become less realistic as open-systems increase in size and less of the information is available locally.

There is a similarity between open-systems characteristics and the distributed problem-solving philosophy of artificial intelligence (Section 3.2.2.1). Open-architecture intelligent systems can be placed under the umbrella of distributed problems-solving. However there are certain differences in the general thrust of distributed problem-solving and open-system approaches. These differences are now discussed.

4.1.2 Distributed Problem-Solving and Open-Systems Approach

A key characteristic in distributed problem-solving of both the "task-sharing" and the "result-sharing" modes of cooperation is the ability to initially characterize the abstraction levels involved in the problem to be solved. The problem is then accordingly subdivided/decomposed into subproblems wherein each abstraction level corresponds to a subproblem which also is an autonomous intelligent system. The focus is on how the knowledge will be organized and how the control among autonomous intelligent systems will take place. Hence there is greater concern with the "content" of the information to be communicated between autonomous intelligent systems, than with the "form" in which the communication is effected [Davis & Smith, 1983].

The open-systems approach is more general in that the main concern is not on how a problem will be subdivided into autonomous intelligent systems, but rather on how a set of autonomous intelligent systems will communicate for problem-solving. Each autonomous intelligent system can be a full problem or a subproblem. The focus is not on the control among autonomous intelligent systems as these systems may not correspond to a specific abstraction level of problem. Hence there is concern with both the "form" and "content" of communication, since the autonomous intelligent systems may not be aware of each others existence and capabilities. So the mode and form of communication in the open-systems approach is more critical for problem-solving.

Now, there are 3 modes in which communication is performed among autonomous intelligent systems in distributed problem-solving:

4.1.2.1. Direct Communication

This type of communication usually takes place when the autonomous intelligent systems are created on the basis of some hierarchy or planning. Here the autonomous intelligent systems are aware of "with whom" and "what" they have to communicate. The planning involved in the creation of autonomous intelligent systems also acts as a basis of control and synthesis of results [Li, 1987; Evans, 1988].

4.1.2.2. Broadcast Communication

This type of communication takes place when an autonomous intelligent system does not have a pre-defined plan of the other autonomous intelligent systems which should be contacted for doing work. So a particular autonomous intelligent system then broadcasts a message specifying the "content" of the work to be done, to all the other autonomous intelligent systems. Depending on the response to the broadcast announcement negotiations are conducted and accordingly, an autonomous intelligent system is selected [Smith, 1981; Smith & Davis, 1983].

4.1.2.3. Indirect Communication

This type of communication involves sending the "content" of communication to a common data structure. The common structure then monitors and controls the problem-solving activity. The autonomous intelligent systems are not aware of "with whom" they should communicate [Erman *et al.*, 1980].

Due to the general nature of open-systems, the broadcast communication mode is closest in addressing the needs of the open-systems communication requirements. But since in open-systems, no autonomous intelligent system need be aware of other autonomous systems that can cooperate for problem-solving, broadcasting on its own will always be very cumbersome. What is necessary is a communication mode that is not simply broadcasting but also has a specific purpose and intention attached to the "content". This purpose and intention involved in a communication mode would improve the handling of the "content" of the communication by the receiving autonomous intelligent system.

As communication is paramount in the open-systems approach to intelligent information system, it is essential to have a problem-solving framework (conceptual architecture) that reduces the unnecessary communication among the involved autonomous intelligent systems by focusing on where the communication should be addressed as soon as possible.

4.1.3 Elements of an Open-Systems Architecture

There are four major elements involved in an open-systems approach to systems development which a conceptual architecture should cater to:

1. The existence of multiple autonomous intelligent subsystems.
2. The provision for communication among such autonomous intelligent subsystems.
3. The coherence of behaviour of the various autonomous intelligent subsystems for achieving a solution.
4. The descriptors to model the structure of objects in an intelligent subsystem.

These elements are now discussed in the context of open-system properties and the characteristics specified earlier.

Intelligent systems based on the open-systems principle would be comprised of a number of autonomous intelligent subsystems. Each such intelligent subsystem would have its own self-knowledge, and be limited to its domain only. There would be no global objects, and so it may become difficult to determine what objects exist at any point in time in different intelligent subsystems of the overall system. Consequently, the ''closed world assumption'' may not be applicable in a system built using this approach.

Therefore, instead of a single huge organization-wide knowledge base [Bubenko, 1983], there would be smaller knowledge bases attached to the multitude of autonomous intelligent subsystems. Each autonomous intelligent subsystem would now represent some functional expertise in the organization thereby providing a basis for "partitioning" the overall organizational knowledge base.

As there are no global objects, the only thing that the various intelligent subsystems hold in common is the ability to communicate with each other. Emphasis is no negotiations among the intelligent subsystems. Much of the communication will be on the basis of "dissemination", i.e. once a piece of knowledge is disseminated (communicated), other knowledge in the receiving intelligent subsystem might be affected. Hence the communication or message passing semantics should take the meaning of a message to be the effect it has on the subsequent behaviour of the system, i.e. how it affects the recipient intelligent subsystem.

Intelligent systems based on the open-systems approach will be inherently modular in structure as their development can be incremental and non-hierarchial. Since there are no global objects and schemas, one can initially define and implement a few urgent intelligent subsystems and later incorporate other intelligent subsystems, without any impact on existing intelligent subsystems. Also as knowledge is added to an intelligent subsystem it must relate to its existing knowledge only.

Now as any intelligent subsystem can have only partial knowledge of the overall system, it only has partial power to affect other intelligent subsystems. Open-systems intelligent systems must have mechanisms to achieve "coherence" of behaviour, i.e. convergence in a set of negotiations [Brady, 1982]. Starting negotiations/communications is only the beginning; mechanisms must be developed for bringing them to successful conclusions [Davis & Smith, 1981]. These mechanisms should specify how the control among intelligent subsystems will exist, and which intelligent subsystem will have the ultimate responsibility for the generation of problem solution.

To make open-architecture intelligent systems feasible it is necessary to provide for appropriate "descriptors" to facilitate the conceptual modelling of the objects and properties in the various autonomous intelligent subsystems. It is contended that the descriptors should be defined by a rigorous mathematical semantics [Attardi & Simi, 1981] and should have an epistemological basis that is compatible with the realities being modelled. Also descriptors should provide for "due process" reasoning, i.e. mechanisms for gathering evidence in parallel from parties affected by an issue, weighing the evidence, and then making a decision. Understanding due process reasoning is central to modelling the reasoning processes that go in open-systems. For this reason descriptors should have good communication capabilities.

Few (if any) working intelligent information systems have been constructed based on the open-system approach. Part of the reason for the lack of such open-architecture systems has been the non-existence of a compatible conceptual architecture.

4.2 CONCEPTUAL DESIGN OF THE OIIS ARCHITECTURE

The open-systems approach premise is that the overall intelligent information system should comprise many small autonomous intelligent subsystems which would have been developed separately and independently, and that these autonomous intelligent subsystems should automatically communicate with each other for problem-solving. The key attributes of the open-systems approach, viz. 'intelligent subsystems creation' and 'communication among intelligent subsystems', form the underlying theme for the proposed development of the conceptual architecture, called the Open Intelligent Information Systems (OIIS) architecture. A major objective of an OIIS architecture is to provide an appropriate communications capability enabling the autonomous intelligent systems to properly cooperate in problem-solving.

Now since formal languages have formed the basis for the creation of knowledge bases conventionally, such languages I feel should also be utilized to provide the capability for the various autonomous intelligent subsystems to communicate and integrate for problem-solving. I believe that an appropriate starting point for this new architecture is human language. For this reason I have chosen speech act theory as my starting point. However speech act theory has been subsequently transformed into a close equivalent, which I call message acts. These message acts ultimately provide the standard and formal semantic-driven protocol for communication among autonomous intelligent subsystems.

In summary, the basic approach to designing an OIIS architecture is to partition the entire intelligent information system into different autonomous intelligent subsystems, wherein each knowledge-module is an autonomous intelligent system. These autonomous intelligent subsystems communicate with each other to get the overall intelligent system working. Message act concepts from the basis for communication among the autonomous intelligent subsystems. The use and construction of message acts brings a natural orderliness to the development of intelligent information systems. An outline of the fundamentals of the

OIIS architecture is now provided before going into the details of speech acts and message acts.

4.2.1 Fundamentals of the Architecture

The components of an open intelligent information system architecture are shown in Figure 4.1. These components have the following characteristics that enable the development of the OIIS:

1. Instead of having a single knowledge base, the entire intelligent systems knowledge is partitioned into different and smaller knowledge bases. These smaller knowledge bases enable the creation of individual autonomous intelligent subsystems. Having such separate autonomous intelligent subsystems helps reduce complexity and bring modularity in the development process.
2. The overall intelligent system may have a single user-interface if such an OIIS corresponds to a single entity/organization. In a geographically distributed environment each autonomous intelligent subsystem will have its own user-interface.
3. The user-interface will interact with the relevant autonomous intelligent subsystem's inference engine before accessing the knowledge base.
4. There will be a module called the *concept dictionary*, with which all autonomous intelligent subsystems and the user-interface will interact. This dictionary is a compendium of the various concepts handled by the different autonomous intelligent subsystems of the OIIS.
5. There will also be module called the *communications dictionary*, which will contain the generalized procedures for the execution of message acts.
6. Use of specific message acts by any autonomous intelligent subsystem will be embedded in the knowledge-rules of its knowledge base. Whenever specific work has to be done from the other autonomous intelligent subsystems, the calling autonomous intelligent subsystem will generate the specific message act to the called autonomous intelligent subsystem.
7. Communication between the autonomous intelligent subsystems will always be through the communications dictionary. In other

words, logically the autonomous intelligent subsystems will seem to be communicating with each other directly, but physically all such communication will be through the communications dictionary.

8. Whenever any autonomous intelligent subsystem desires to know which concept is being handled by which other autonomous intelligent subsystem, it will access the concept dictionary.

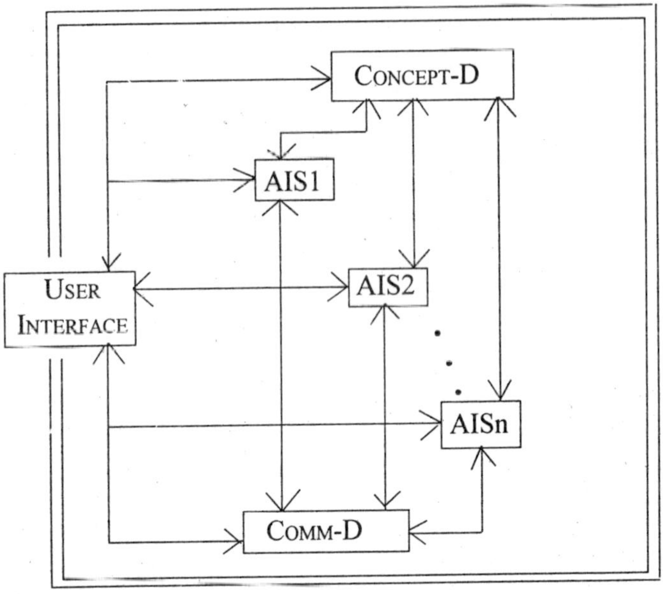

LEGEND:

AIS1 : Autonomous intelligent subsystem
CONCEPT-D : Concept Dictionary
COMM-D : Communications Dictionary

FIG 4.1: Open Intelligent Information Systems Architecture

9. The inference engine of each autonomous intelligent subsystem will determine the control strategy for the handling of an autonomous intelligent subsystem's knowledge base and finding solutions.

10. Users can specify their interaction with the OIIS through the user-interface in the following ways:

    (a) Specify a predicate (concept) as a basis for question or confirmation of some work.

    (b) Specify the message act directly as a basis for updating the knowledge base of any autonomous intelligent subsystem.

    (c) Delete any knowledge from the knowledge base of an autonomous intelligent subsystem. (This feature is due to operational reasons-keeping the disk space manageable).

11. As each autonomous intelligent subsystem is an intelligent system in itself, it can have its own knowledge representation scheme for representing knowledge. In such a multiple knowledge representation environment, the inference engine of the autonomous intelligent subsystem will have the responsibility of transforming the external knowledge format to its internal format and vice-versa when communicating externally.

4.2.2 Theoretical Foundations for Communication in OIIS

The theory of speech acts (SACTS) proposed by Searle [Searle, 1969] forms the basis for the communication protocols. SACTS is a generalization of the human linguistic communications which are performed by the utterance of sentences. As organizations are also perceived as networks of commitments and communication [Mintzberg, 1973; Winograd & Flores, 1987], SACTS relevancy in organizational contexts cannot be denied.

A speech act involves four aspects:

1. An utterance act.
2. A proposition act.
3. An illocutionary act.
4. A perlocutionary act.

The uttering of an expression is called an utterance act.

Every sentence/expression will have a proposition within it, i.e. it must be referring to and predicating on some fact about the sentence/

expression. Such an aspect is called a proposition act.

The intention with which the speaker utters the sentence is referred to as an illocutionary act.

The speaking of a sentence/expression will have some consequence or effect on the actions, thoughts, beliefs, and so on of the hearer. Such aspects are called the perlocutionary acts.

In performing an illocutionary act, one characteristically performs utterance acts and proposition acts. In an illocutionary act the nature of the consequences are not part of the act. Besides, in the real world there is little control over the consequences. Hence a perlocutionary act may be independent of the illocutionary act. Propositional acts cannot occur alone, i.e. one cannot simply refer and predicate (like assert) without having an intention (like assertion or question) or making an illocutionary act.

Illocutionary acts can be classified into five categories based on the social relationships:

1. The *assertive act*, i.e. the speaker presents a proposition as representing an actual state of affairs.

   e.g. the price of the product *X* is *Y*.

2. The *commissive act,* i.e. the speaker commits itself to a certain course of action represented by the propositional content.

   e.g. we shall fulfil your order number *Z* in two weeks.

3. The *directive act*, i.e. the speaker's attempt is to get the hearer to commit itself to a certain course of action represented by the propositional content.

   e.g. we order product *X* in quantity *Y*.

4. The *declarative act*, i.e. the speaker produces the state of affairs represented by the propositional content solely by the successful performance of the speech act.

   e.g. we classify you as a credit customer.

5. The *expressive act*, i.e. the speaker discloses psychological states and attitudes about the state of affairs represented by the propositional content.

   e.g. we express to you our gratitude that your orders have increased 20 per cent this year.

According to Searle [Searle, 1976], intention is a representation of states or objects real or imagined, and intentionality relates the intender to these objects and conditions. Thus, describing an intention also means specifying the object or state of affairs which is represented in the intention.

Searle's taxonomy depends on delimiting the universe of classifiable acts to those which are illocutionary--whose effects are achievable almost automatically upon utterance, through the shared rules of meaning. These acts and their corresponding effects define the range of linguistic meaning. Further effects, achieved as the consequences of these acts are not part of the taxonomy because they rely on a further act by the hearer pursuant to comprehension, and thus are not part of purely linguistic intentions and effects which are achievable merely by using the norms of language and therefore are describable by rules [Reiss, 1985].

The further perlocutionary goals (achieved 'through' speaking, not merely 'by' speaking), remains in the background of the taxonomy as typical *extra-linguistic* goals associated with illocutionary acts. Thus in Austin's [Austin, 1962] and Searle's [Searle, 1969; Searle, 1979] formulation there is a split between speech act and hearer's response which is mediated by an act of evaluation [Reiss, 1985].

It has been argued that Searle's analytic distinction between illocutionary and perlocutionary effects is artificial and over-refined in excluding the intended extra-linguistic effects from the representation of an illocutionary act. Such extra-linguistic effects have also been referred as *intended perlocutionary effects* (IPE) [Mohan, 1974; Dore, 1977]. By associating IPE as an essential and integral part of an illocutionary act, all the five speech acts have been redefined [Reiss, 1985].

Including the intended perlocutionary effect in the illocutionary intentions, a speaker, in using an illocutionary act, intends to achieve three kinds of effects:

1. The successful expression of a psychological state.
2. The intention to get the hearer to understand this expression.
3. The intention to get the hearer to behave in some designated and conventionalizable way (IPE).

This new encompassing version of SACT has been formulated by Reiss [Reiss, 1985] as follows:

Assertives: The IPE here is that the hearer acts upon the belief expressed by the speaker. The speaker's belief is binding on the hearer.

Commissives: The IPE here is that the hearer acts upon the speaker's expectation. This expectation is not binding on the hearer. Hence the hearer may accept or further act on this expectation now or in the future.

Declaratives: The IPE here is that the hearer accept the facts expressed by the speaker, and may further act on this fact.

Directives: The IPE here is the compliance of the hearer with the action suggested by the speaker, thereby implicating the hearer as an agent to fit the speakers world.

Expressives: The IPE here is that the hearer acts upon his acceptance of the attitudes expressed by the speaker.

Research on the utilization of speech acts in information systems [Lyytinen & Lehtinen, 1986] and artificial intelligence [Cohen & Perrault, 1979; Allen & Perrault, 1980] has already been attempted. Even though speech acts could never be fully represented in computers, researchers still hope it can be used as a basis for speech understanding or some form of natural language interface [Charniak & McDermott, 1987; Nilsson, 1980], or as a formal language for business communications [Kimbrough & Lee, 1986; Winograd & Flores, 1987].

Validity of the speech acts in information systems is part of the language action approach to information system development [Lyytinen, 1986]. Speech act effectiveness was one of the objectives of the SAMPO project [Lyytinen & Lehtinen,1983].

4.2.3 Syntax and Semantics for Communication in OIIS

The communication that we require will occur not between humans but between the autonomous intelligent subsystems of the overall intelligent information system. Consequently, speech acts have been transformed into their close equivalents, which I have called as *message acts* (MACTS). These MACTS provide the semantic and syntactic rules for communication among autonomous intelligent subsystems. Each message act has a semantic connotation, which distinguishes it from other computer communication protocols.

There are two factors involved in message acts (MACTS) development:

1. There should be a proper identification of the relationship among the set of possible MACTS with the corresponding SACTS. Such a relationship would then provide a basis for classifying the MACTS. This classification should further state the conditions that involve the speaker's intentions with the hearer's reactions and the general inferential process.
2. Under what situations would a speaker choose a specific MACT, thereby enabling a specific behaviour in the hearer and the system.

The general format of a message act is:

Operator (Speaker, Hearer, Action)

where *Operator* is a particular revised SACT or a classified illocutionary act; *Speaker* is the sender (KS) of the message; *Hearer* is the receiver (KS) of the message; *Action* is the specific action(s) that *Speaker* wants *Hearer* to either perform or know about.

For a successful communication to take place between the speaker and the hearer it is important that each has the other in a list. This means that the speaker should be aware of the various hearer(s) with whom it is possible to communicate. Also 'when' to call will depend upon the requirements of the speaker. This is an issue which should be resolved at the knowledge acquisition stage. The speaker and hearer are interchangeable, depending upon the requirement.

The various message acts and the action(s) proposed or undertaken by them are as follows:

1. Assert (S, H, Action)

This corresponds to the assertive illocutionary act and its IPE. *S* presents some state of affairs (Action). It tells to *H* how the world is, and orders it to change its world accordingly. *H* will have to act on *S's* belief expressed through this Action.
e.g. the price of product *X* is *Y*.

2. Inform (S, H, Action)

This corresponds to the commissive and declarative illocutionary acts and their IPEs. *S* commits itself to certain course of action (Action) and wants *H* to be aware of it. Here *S* is doing some work (Action) and *H* is simply informed about it. *H* will record the Action, but may also react

to the information provided by *S*.
e.g. the order shall be fulfilled in two weeks.
e.g. we classify you as a credit customer.

3. Request (S, H, Action)

This corresponds to the directive illocutionary act and its IPE. *S* requests *H* to undertake some course of action (Action) and reply.
e.g. can we order product *X* in quantity *Y*.

4. Gratitude (S, H, Action)

This corresponds to the expressive illocutionary act and its IPE. Here *S* is expressing some gratitude or disappointment to *H* on some work done by *H*. *H* does not have to record the operation. Action could be thanks, sorry, etc.
e.g. thanks on the occasion of having orders increased by 20 per cent.

4.3 DISCUSSION OF KEY ADVANCES

Artificial intelligence through intelligent information systems is a simulation of the intelligent working methodology of human beings. Any such simulation cannot ignore the fact that communication is one of the basic tenets on which human knowledge and working is built, expanded and propagated. The OIIS architecture uses this basic idea for the partitioning of the organization's knowledge base. This approach has the promise that knowledge-based systems could be successfully built in a structured and modular manner. The proposed architecture brings many advantages to the information processing area.

Initially it allows the development of information processing systems in a modular and non-hierarchial manner, i.e. in any desired order. In this way, a few urgent parts (autonomous intelligent subsystems) of the organization's UoD can be initially defined and implemented, while the remaining parts can be incorporated in any order later on. This enables an incremental developmental of systems.

Also the architecture provides a standardization of the communication semantics on the basis of which open-systems like architectures would be made more feasible. Of course as the OIIS architecture suggests, if each subsystem is an intelligent system, more advantages can be gained.

An important characteristic of the architecture is its basis for an effective partitioning of the overall knowledge base of the UoD. This subsequently provides a structured knowledge-based approach to intelligent information system development.

The development of open intelligent information systems, it is felt, could also provide insights and understanding of how humans interact during problem-solving. This understanding could aid in the future systems development effort considerably.

Obviously an architecture for OIIS also provides another approach to distributed problem-solving. The distributed problem-solving premise of allowing an autonomous group of agents (intelligent systems) to cooperatively solve problems can be appropriately implemented in OIIS. This can be conceptually done by confining each agent to an autonomous intelligent subsystem, and then allowing such agents to communicate for problem-solving.

A significant outcome of the OIIS architecture is to also provide a means for interconnecting existing multiple intelligent systems, that have different, but possibly overlapping expertise. Obviously this enables the generation of solutions to problems whose domains are outside that of any one intelligent system.

In developing intelligent systems where the overall broader expertise lies not with a single expert, but with several experts or non-experts, it is important to have good conceptual architectures that can provide mechanisms for integrating and representing the overall expertise of the system. This becomes overtly true when experts exist for narrow domains only. OIIS and its conceptual architecture go a long way in providing a proper foundation.

Lastly from the implementation standpoint, OIIS, with its compatible architecture, provides increased reliability. Since each autonomous intelligent subsystem is an intelligent system, the overall system should be theoretically able to operate even if a part (autonomous intelligent subsystem) fails.

5

OIIS ARCHITECTURE IMPLEMENTATION

The validity of the proposed OIIS architecture is demonstrated by a prototype of business situations/cases based on the Order Processing System book case [Gane & Sarson, 1979]. Along with the details of the business cases, implementation details of the concepts and issues relevant to the OIIS architecture are also discussed. The entire implementation was done in the Prolog language (VMPROLOG of IBM) on an IBM 4381 system. The complete program listings are provided in the appendix at the end of the dissertation. The various assumptions made and the limitations of the proposed implementation are also provided for a proper perspective on the extent of this OIIS architectural implementation. The knowledge representation scheme used for this implementation is 'production rules'. The chapter first discusses the OIIS case that has been implemented and then describes the implementation of the architectural concepts.

5.1 DESCRIPTION OF THE OIIS CASE STUDY

The case study is an illustration of an OIIS dealing with pre-specified situations. Before going into the details of the case implementation, a brief overview is provided.

5.1.1 Overview of the Case

The case deals with sample business situations arising from the interactions among three business functional areas autonomous intelligent subsystems, viz. marketing, accounting and inventory. The autonomous intelligent subsystems for these functional areas are supposedly developed independently of each other, i.e. there is no global schema. Each autonomous intelligent subsystem specifies procedures for completing its specific operations. However in order to complete these operations some knowledge may be needed from another functional area autonomous intelligent subsystems. For this purpose a functional area autonomous intelligent subsystem simply needs to be aware of the 'concept' that will provide the necessary knowledge. How the 'concept' is worked upon by the other functional area autonomous intelligent subsystems is not essential.

All functional area autonomous intelligent subsystems have various 'rules' and 'facts' in their knowledge base to handle the specific business situations. For the successful completion of a particular rule, if the need for interaction with other autonomous intelligent subsystems is required, appropriate message acts are issued. In other words, message acts are part of the body of the rule in the knowledge base of an autonomous intelligent subsystem.

In this implementation case study, knowledge in the knowledge bases of the functional area autonomous intelligent subsystems is centered around the processing of a hypothetical concept 'order' for some product. The products are named prod1, prod2 and prod3. The autonomous intelligent subsystem that is first invoked and responsible for the problem-solving or completion of processing is the marketing autonomous intelligent subsystem. This autonomous intelligent subsystem is responsible for handling the order, for which it may have to interact with the accounting or inventory autonomous intelligent subsystems. The concept 'order' needs information on customer name, product name, quantity of the product and the date of placing the order before processing any further. For instance, mkt: order (john, prod1, 30, 3/10/89) implies that there is an order by customer 'john' for '30' units of the product named 'prod1' and the date of placing the order is 3/10/89.

5.1.2 Operational Details of the Case

There are five scenarios which are handled by the autonomous intelligent subsystems involved with a product order. These scenarios are now discussed in detail along with the associated diagrams. During the scenario narrative, the predicate names associated with the concept involved are mentioned in parenthesis along with their respective autonomous intelligent subsystem. For instance, mkt: order refers to the 'order' predicate in the marketing autonomous intelligent subsystem. The accounting and inventory autonomous intelligent subsystems are referred as 'acct' and 'inv' respectively. Implementation details can be found in the program listing in Appendix-A. The reasoning used and the solution space for each scenario as performed under the OIIS architecture is provided in Appendix-B.

Scenario 1

The order (mkt: order) arrives at the marketing autonomous intelligent subsystem. The subsystem finds that the customer is an old client of the company (mkt: cust_type) and so a 'request' is made to the accounting autonomous intelligent subsystem to find out the financial status of the customer (acct: cust_fin_status). The accounting autonomous intelligent subsystem replies with a report of good financial standing relative to the customers previous payments to the company. Now, the marketing autonomous intelligent subsystem makes the necessary detailed entries for the order (mkt: order_details_entry) and 'informs' the accounting autonomous intelligent subsystem that it is ready to send the order for shipment (acct: cust_ord). Then the marketing autonomous intelligent subsystem 'asserts' to the inventory autonomous intelligent subsystem the instructions to ship the order (inv: prod_ship) to the customer. The inventory autonomous intelligent subsystem first balances its stock for the particular product (inv: prod_stock) and, seeing that a sufficient quantity exists, goes about loading the order for shipment (inv: prod_load). Once the order has been loaded for shipment, the inventory autonomous intelligent subsystem 'informs' both the marketing autonomous intelligent subsystem and the accounting autonomous intelligent subsystem about this development (mkt: order_shipped and acct: order_shipped). The accounting autonomous intelligent subsystem on receiving this new piece of knowledge issues the invoice for the order (acct: acct_ord_ship).

Example: order (john, prod1, 10,2/12/88) in file 'WHY1 OUT' listing.

The scenario is illustrated in Figure 5.1.

Scenario 2

The order (mkt: order) arrives at the marketing autonomous intelligent subsystem. The subsystem finds that the customer is an old client of the

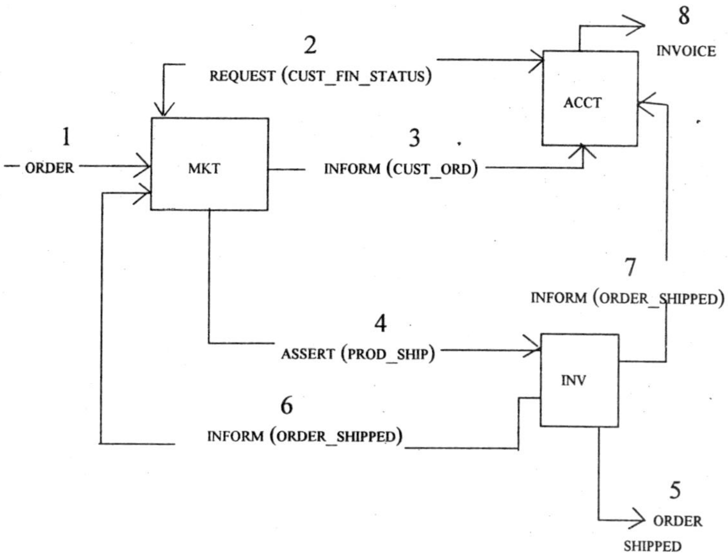

FIG. 5.1

company (mkt: cust_type) and so a 'request' is made to the accounting autonomous intelligent subsystem to find out the financial status of the customer (acct: cust_fin_status). The accounting autonomous intelligent subsystem replies with a report of bad financial standing relative to the customer's previous payments to the company. Now, the marketing autonomous intelligent subsystem checks the quantity ordered for the product against some critical standard quantity (mkt: prod_critical_value). If the result is negative, then the marketing autonomous intelligent subsystem determines that the customer needs to make some advance payment along with the order. Otherwise, if the result is positive, a 'request' is made to the accounting autonomous intelligent subsystem for further credit status information on the customer (acct: cust_credit_status). If the credit status of the customer is satisfactory, the marketing autonomous intelligent subsystem goes ahead with the further detailed processing of the order (mkt: order_details_entry), and then 'informs' the accounting autonomous intelligent subsystem that it is sending the order for shipment entailing a small risk (acct: cust_ord). Then, the marketing autonomous intelligent subsystem 'asserts' to the inventory autonomous intelligent subsystem the instructions to ship the order (inv: prod_ship) to the customer. The inventory autonomous intelligent subsystem first balances its stock for the particular product (inv: prod_stock) and, seeing that a sufficient quantity exists, goes about loading the order for shipment (inv: prod_load). Once the order has been loaded for shipment, the inventory autonomous intelligent subsystem 'informs' both the marketing autonomous intelligent subsystem and the accounting autonomous intelligent subsystem about this development (mkt: order_shipped and acct: order_shipped). The accounting autonomous intelligent subsystem on receiving this new piece of knowledge issues the invoice for the order (acct: acct_ord_ship).

Example: order (jack, prod3, 10, 3/15/89) in file 'WHY2 OUT' listing.

order (jack, prod2, 20, 3/15/89) in file 'WHY2A OUT' listing.

This scenario is illustrated in Figure 5.2 and Figure 5.3.

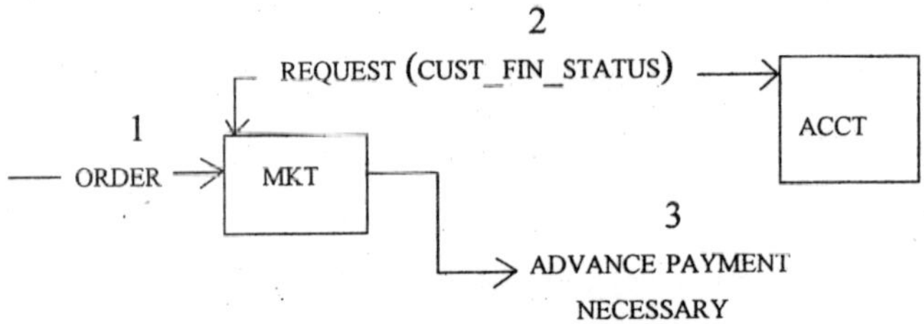

FIG. 5.2

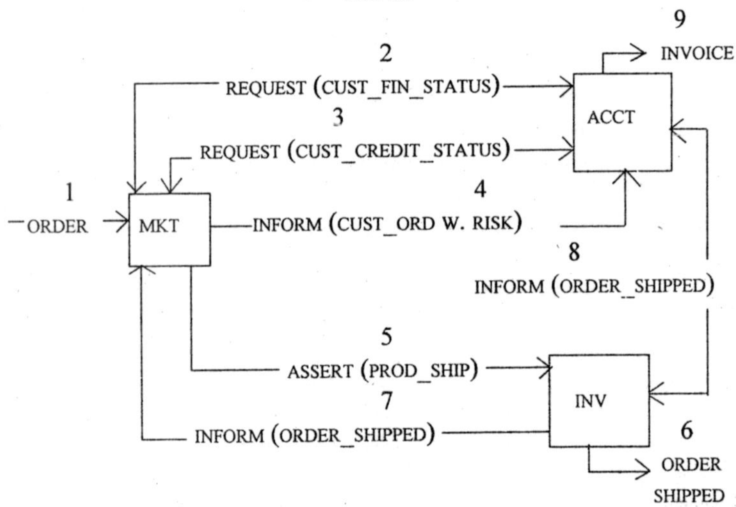

FIG. 5.3

Scenario 3

The order (mkt: order) arrives at the marketing autonomous intelligent subsystem. The subsystem finds that the customer is a new client of the company (mkt: cust_type). Accordingly, the customer is assigned a new customer number (mkt: gen_cust_no) and then the accounting autonomous intelligent subsystem is 'informed' about it (acct: new_cust). The accounting autonomous intelligent subsystem now generates the credit limits for the new customer (acct: gen_credit_limits). Thereafter, the marketing autonomous intelligent subsystem makes the necessary detailed entries (mkt: order_details_entry) and 'informs' the accounting autonomous intelligent subsystem that it is ready to send the order for shipment (acct: cust_ord). Then the marketing autonomous intelligent subsystem 'asserts' to the inventory autonomous intelligent subsystem the instructions to ship the order to the customer (inv: prod_ship). The inventory autonomous intelligent subsystem first balances its stock for the particular product (inv: prod_stock) and, seeing that a sufficient quantity exists, goes about loading the order for shipment (inv: prod_load). Once the order has been loaded for shipment, the inventory autonomous intelligent subsystem 'informs' both the marketing autonomous intelligent subsystem and the accounting autonomous intelligent subsystem about this development (mkt: order_shipped and acct: order_shipped). The accounting autonomous intelligent subsystem on receiving this new piece of knowledge issues the invoice for the order (acct: acct_ord_ship).

Example: order (alan, prod2, 10, 3/15/88) in file 'WHY3 OUT' listing.

The scenario is illustrated in Figure 5.4.

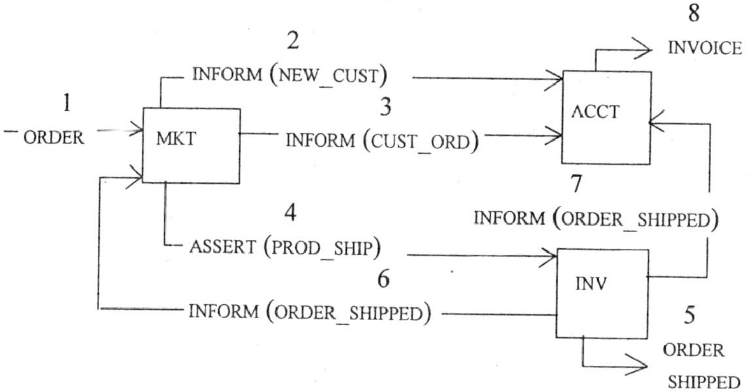

FIG. 5.4

Scenario 4

The order (mkt: order) arrives at the marketing autonomous intelligent subsystem. The subsystem finds that the customer is a new client of the company (mkt: cust_type). Accordingly the customer is assigned a new customer number (mkt: gen_cust_no) and then the accounting autonomous intelligent subsystem is 'informed' about it (acct: new_cust). The accounting autonomous intelligent subsystem now generates the credit limits for the customer (acct: gen_credit_limits). Thereafter, the marketing autonomous intelligent subsystem makes the necessary detailed entries (mkt: order_details_entry) and 'informs' the accounting autonomous intelligent subsystem that it is ready to send the order for shipment (acct: cust_ord). Now the accounting autonomous intelligent subsystem invokes the rule for checking the customer credit status (acct: cust_credit_status) and finds that the customer's general credit standing is bad and so accordingly 'informs' the marketing autonomous intelligent subsystem about it (mkt: cust_credit_status). The marketing autonomous intelligent subsystem on receiving this piece of knowledge decides to change the order details of the customer (mkt: cust_credit_standing) from normal to pending, and requests advance payment from the customer before further processing of the order.

Example: order (terry, prod2, 10, 4/12/88) in file 'WHY4 OUT' listing.

The scenario is illustrated in Figure 5.5.

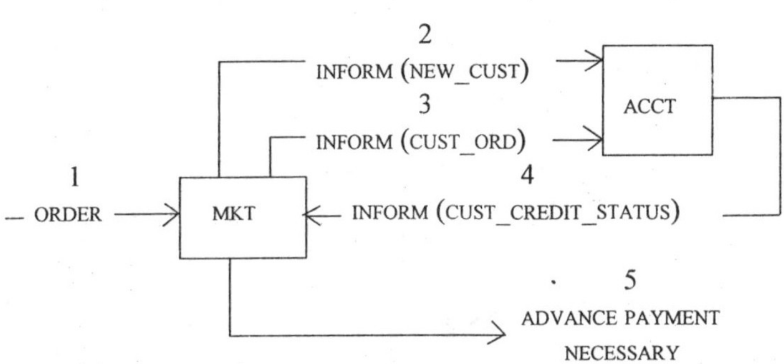

FIG.5.5

Scenario 5

The order (mkt: order) arrives at the marketing autonomous intelligent subsystem. The subsystem finds the type of customer (mkt: cust_type) and accordingly completes its internal processing as specified in scenario 1 and scenario 3. Then the marketing autonomous intelligent subsystem 'asserts' to the inventory autonomous intelligent subsystem the instructions to ship to order to the customer (inv: prod_ship). The inventory autonomous intelligent subsystem finds that the product stock has a low quantity of the item ordered (inv: prod_stock) and so 'informs' the marketing autonomous intelligent subsystem that the order has been placed on a normal pending list (mkt: order_pending). The marketing autonomous intelligent subsystem finds on receiving this information from the inventory autonomous intelligent subsystem that the customer is important to the company (mkt: cust_imp) and so it next 'asserts' to the inventory autonomous intelligent subsystem the instruction to increase the waiting priority of this order (inv: order_prior_chg).

Example: order (mary, prod3, 60, 4/15/89) in file 'WHY5 OUT' listing.

The scenario is illustrated in Figure 5.6.

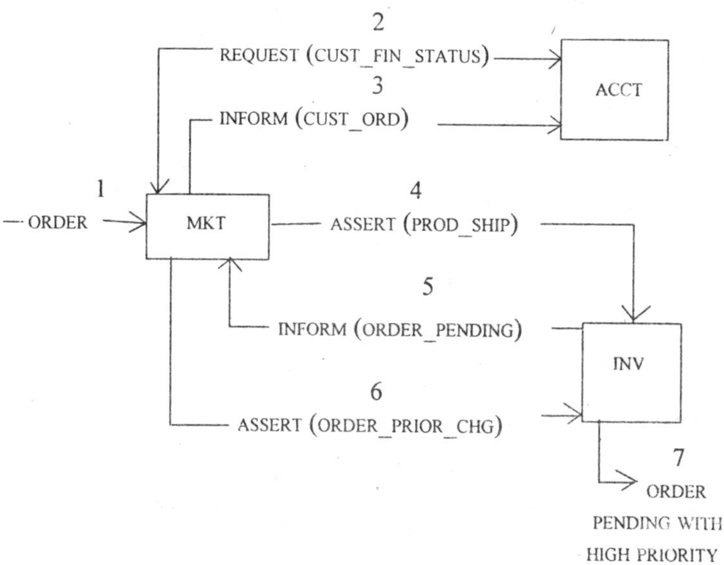

FIG. 5.6

5.2 DESCRIPTION OF THE OIIS ARCHITECTURE DETAILS

The conceptual details of the architecture described here are general for any OIIS implementation. However due to the use of VMPROLOG for developing the OIIS case, the implementation is slightly biased toward the syntax of Prolog.

There is no limit on the number of autonomous intelligent subsystems that can be supported by the OIIS architecture. Each autonomous intelligent subsystem can be designed independently. In this implementation all production rules have a prefix, viz. 'mkt' for marketing, 'acct' for accounting, 'inv' for inventory, which reflects their respective functional areas. The autonomous intelligent subsystem designers will have to access the concept-dictionary to find the different concepts handled by the other knowledge systems. Accordingly the communication aspects should be incorporated into the building of the knowledge bases. This communication feature based on message acts and their implementation in the communications-dictionary will depend upon the way the designers perceive that knowledge from other knowledge modules may be best utilized.

The existing functionality of the OIIS case has already been described in section 5.1. The details of the knowledge in the different knowledge bases will vary among organizations, reflecting each organization's way of working. However there are some technical architectural characteristics that will enable the proper working of such open-systems. These technical features are:

1. Structure of entries in the concept dictionary.
2. Structure of entries in the communications dictionary.
3. Structure of the inference engine.

Each of the above aspects are discussed in detail in the remainder of this section.

5.2.1 Structure of Concept Dictionary

The purpose of entries in the concept dictionary is to provide a particular autonomous intelligent subsystem with the names of other autonomous intelligent subsystems that are capable of handling a particular concept. It is like an index which gives the name of another autonomous intelligent be capable of handling a particular concept. The prolog language syntax of the entries comprising the concept dictionary is:

com: com (Concept_Name, Knowledge_Module).

e.g. com: com (cust_fin_status, acct).

Concept dictionary entries are shown in the program listing in Appendix-A.

Provisions for handling 'aliases' are not provided in this implementation, but could be included. Aliases would imply giving the same concept different predicate names by the various autonomous intelligent subsystems. It will be the responsibility of the autonomous intelligent subsystem interacting with the concept dictionary to appropriately decide among the different aliases. The concept dictionary will maintain in such cases a list of different predicate names corresponding to a particular concept.

Also it is possible that the same concept can be handled by more than one autonomous intelligent subsystem. In this case again, it is the responsibility of the interacting autonomous intelligent subsystem to decide on the particular autonomous intelligent subsystem to work with. It is assumed that all the autonomous intelligent subsystems are aware of the number of arguments that need to be passed to a predicate (concept) when it is invoked.

5.2.2 Structure of Communication Dictionary

The communication dictionary is comprised of message acts which enable communication between any two autonomous intelligent subsystems. The logical structure and the semantic context of message acts has already been specified earlier. Here, the physical structure in the VMPROLOG language syntax is provided. Communication dictionary entries are also shown in the program listing in Appendix-A.

All message acts as specified earlier will have three arguments, viz. Speaker, Hearer and Action. The Speaker argument pertains to the autonomous intelligent subsystem that is attempting to communicate. The Hearer argument pertains to the autonomous intelligent subsystem that is being called. The Action argument consists of some proper predicate (concept) that specifies the work for the Hearer autonomous intelligent subsystem to execute. The predicate in the Action argument refers to the concept/predicate name identified in the concept-dictionary. It is expected that the Speaker will check with the concept dictionary to find the Hearer autonomous intelligent subsystems that can handle the particular concept. Although the syntax of the message act predicate will remain the same, it is the structure of the predicate in the Action argument and the work that is expected from the Hearer autonomous intelligent subsystem in handling this predicate that will distinguish these message acts. Accordingly the discussion of message act focuses on the structure and nature of work of the predicate in the Action argument.

The ASSERT message act would be implemented as:
mact: assert (Speaker, Hearer, Action) ← call (Hearer: Action).

All arguments in the Action predicate must be non-variables. The presence of non-variable arguments in the Action predicate is an attempt to force the Hearer autonomous intelligent subsystem to work according to the values provided by the Speaker autonomous intelligent subsystem. In other words, this structure of the Action predicate is to command the Hearer autonomous intelligent subsystem to change its UoD in accordance with the complete values or beliefs of the Speaker autonomous intelligent subsystem. The Hearer autonomous intelligent subsystem in this situation has no alternative but to act by having the appropriate rule invoked.

e.g. mact: assert (mkt, inv, prod_ship (prod1, 21, 20, 31)).

The REQUEST message act would be implemented as:
mact: request (Speaker, Hearer, Action) ← call (Hearer: Action).

Now, the Action predicate must have at least one argument which is a variable. This variable will get instantiated in the Hearer autonomous intelligent subsystem and accordingly return to the Speaker autonomous intelligent subsystem some value representing a reply. In other words, this structure of the Action predicate is to make the Hearer autonomous intelligent subsystem comply with the Speakers world and by replying back make the Hearer autonomous intelligent subsystem implicated completely with the Speakers UoD.

e.g. mact: request (mkt, acct, cust_fin_status (21, Type)).

The INFORM message act would be implemented as:
mact: inform (Speaker, Hearer, Action) ← addax (Hearer: Action).

Here all arguments in the Action predicate must be non-variables.

Having non-variable arguments will fully represent the Speaker autonomous intelligent subsystem's expectations or part of its UoD. This piece of knowledge from the Action is initially always added to Hearer autonomous intelligent subsystem's knowledge base. After this addition of knowledge, the Hearer autonomous intelligent subsystem may further act immediately by initiating a knowledge rule that may need this Action predicate knowledge or it may keep this knowledge for future use. To issue this message act, it is not necessary for the Speaker autonomous intelligent subsystem to check with the concept-dictionary for the name of the Hearer autonomous intelligent subsystem that will handle the Action predicate. This message act can be issued whenever the Speaker autonomous intelligent subsystem feels that it wishes to inform the other autonomous intelligent subsystems of some activity that it has performed or of some aspect of its UoD. It is part of the autonomous intelligent subsystem's design to decide which autonomous intelligent subsystems should be informed of such activity.

e.g. mact: inform (mkt, acct, cust_ord (31, 25, prod1, 20, ok)).

The GRATITUDE message act is not implemented as it does not have much relevance in such automatic machine communication.

5.2.3 Structure of the Inference Engine

Inference engines consist of a set of procedures which follow a pre-determined general inference control strategy that enables the manipulation of the knowledge base for solving given problems. Inference engines usually also have a reasoning mechanism built-in, that explains how and why a particular course of action for the solution space was pursued. There have been three types of inference control strategies that inference engines have generally followed, viz. backward chaining, forward chaining, and mixed chaining (combination of backward and forward chaining).

These strategies, although quite successful with production system or blackboard system architectures, are inadequate from the OIIS architecture perspective. There are some major reasons for the inadequacy of the existing inference control strategies in the OIIS environment, which are discussed below.

5.2.3.1 Reasons for New Inference Control Strategy

OIIS involves the passing of messages among the autonomous intelligent subsystems directly for problem solving and so it is quite possible for the Speaker autonomous intelligent subsystem in one problem to also become the Hearer autonomous intelligent subsystem for some other autonomous intelligent subsystem within the same problem space simultaneously. Thus there can be situations when a particular autonomous intelligent subsystem may at different times be performing the roles of Speaker and Hearer. The existing inference control strategies do not exhibit capabilities to handle such situations for the OIIS.

Also during problem solving, because an autonomous intelligent subsystem may have to act in varied roles as Speaker or Hearer, it is necessary that the consistency of knowledge in the knowledge base be maintained. This implies that the inference engine should ensure that if some piece of knowledge is added when an autonomous intelligent subsystem is the Speaker, then this knowledge is not deleted when the same autonomous intelligent subsystem also becomes the Hearer of some other Speaker autonomous intelligent subsystem. But, retrospectively, this type of scenario also suggests that due to the interaction with other autonomous intelligent subsystems, the existing problem solution space will change, requiring the autonomous intelligent subsystem to delete the same piece of knowledge that it had added earlier on. The likely course in such situations would be for the system to stop further processing and display the reasons for this sudden action. The existing inference control strategies again have no provisions for carrying out such integrity checks.

When an autonomous intelligent subsystem performs the Speaker and Hearer roles at the same time, it is necessary to see that the knowledge rules that were initiated by the autonomous intelligent subsystem as a Speaker are not instantiated again when the same autonomous intelligent subsystem is called as a Hearer (loop structure avoidance). This type of situation would suggest that the offending interactions among the autonomous intelligent subsystems do not actually augment the problem solution space, since the same knowledge rule was invoked again. The likely course in such cases would be for the system to detect this loop and not to invoke the knowledge rule again. The existing inference control strategies due to their inability to handle multiple knowledge systems in the same environment, do not exhibit such capability.

Lastly, whenever a piece of knowledge is added by one autonomous intelligent subsystem to another autonomous intelligent subsystem it may be appropriate to see whether this new knowledge can have any impact in the autonomous intelligent subsystem receiving it. Merely adding a piece of knowledge in the Hearer autonomous intelligent subsystem and letting it remain there may not be contributory to the Speaker autonomous intelligent subsystem. In fact, it is quite possible that the Hearer autonomous intelligent subsystem may already have some other existing knowledge rules that could be invoked and which could in turn improve the solution space for the Speaker autonomous intelligent subsystem. The likely course of action would now be to check if some rule could be instantiated by forward chaining, if the new knowledge does not directly invoke any existing rule. In other words, the inference control strategy apart from handling the above case should also be a mixed one.

5.2.3.2 Development of New Inference Engine

Due to the nature of the OIIS environment and the reasons for the inadequacy of the existing inference strategies cited above, it is imperative that a new inference control strategy (inference engine) be developed. Such an inference control strategy should also be applicable to non-OIIS environments to further improve its versatility. There are two approaches for such inference engine development.

1. Provide different autonomous intelligent subsystems with their own separate inference engines. This would be highly appropriate if the autonomous intelligent subsystems are dispersed among different machines.
2. Have a single inference engine for the entire OIIS. This inference engine will at the time a particular autonomous intelligent subsystem is invoked, behave as if it is working exclusively for this particular autonomous intelligent subsystem.

In this implementation I have taken the second approach by developing a single inference engine for the entire OIIS. This inference engine is invoked when the user through the user-interface enters the predicate 'newexpert' with the problem as its argument. The engine writes its reasoning of the way the problem solution was achieved in the file 'whyshell out'.

e.g. newexpert (mkt: order (john, prod1, 20, 3/15/89)).

A program listing of the inference engine is shown in Appendix-C.

5.3 SUMMARY AND CONCLUSIONS

The OIIS described in Appendix-A consists of three autonomous intelligent subsystems, viz. marketing, accounting and inventory. The knowledge representation scheme used is production rules. Each autonomous intelligent subsystem has its own knowledge base, made distinct by the inclusion of a prefix in the knowledge rule or knowledge fact definition. There are five scenarios which show the working of the system. The reasoning for the solution achieved for each of the scenarios is also provided in Appendix-B.

Due to the unique requirements and structure of an OIIS, a new inference control strategy (inference engine) is proposed. This strategy provides for the interaction among the autonomous intelligent subsystems, while also preserving the integrity of the different knowledge bases as well as avoiding cyclic situations. The inference engine uses a mixed control strategy-basically backward chaining, but in some cases it does forward chaining.

This implementation provides a sample illustration of how the OIIS environment could be realized in real world situations. In spite of some limitations and assumptions that have been specified, the implementation of the OIIS architecture is a major research area which can be further built and improved upon.

6

CONTRIBUTIONS OF THE RESEARCH

The open intelligent information system architecture proposed in this dissertation is a novel way for developing intelligent information processing systems. This architecture is an attempt to bring to fruition the open-systems approach for developing intelligent systems. The previous chapters have provided the theoretical foundations used for structuring and organizing an open intelligent information processing system. Further validation of the architecture has also been demonstrated during its implementation along with issues that need to be addressed for full-scale implementation.

Contributions of this research can be viewed from both the perspective of information processing system theory and information processing system practice. The following section outlines such contributions, after which some directions for further research are provided.

6.1 CONTRIBUTIONS TO INFORMATION PROCESSING SYSTEM THEORY AND PRACTICE

Contributions to information processing system theory and practice stem from the theoretical concepts which underlie the function of the open-systems approach and the consequent open intelligent information system architecture. Some of the major contributions are discussed now.

6.1.1 Open-World System Development

An important contribution that this research makes by the development of the OIIS architecture is the realization of the open-world assumptions for system building. While alternative views and assumptions for system development (like the open-world assumption) have been proposed by other researchers, making them operational has been achieved. The OIIS architecture apart from specifying the conceptual elements relevant for the successful building of an open-system also provides appropriate theoretical foundations for the suggested elements.

6.1.2 Operationalization of Speech Acts

Another contribution of this research has been the operationalization of the speech act theory of language by its modification into message acts and their consequent implementation. This operationalization may not be the ideal adaptation from the philosophical standpoint. However, the research has illustrated how an important theory of language can be utilized in building information processing systems.

6.1.3 Relevancy of Conceptual Architectures

The research also emphasizes the relevancy and importance of conceptual architectures not only in system building, but also in the realization of alternate views/assumptions (like open-systems views) for system development. The conventional focus in system development theory and practice is biased toward the system development methodologies as a basis for developing better systems. Although development methodologies are important for building systems, attention should also be focused on how the various system concepts can be integrated in a conceptual architectural framework. Development of conceptual architectures also enables a proper analysis of the associated methodologies. Attempts can be made to further develop new conceptual architectures which could then provide a basis/guideline for better system methodologies.

6.1.4 Modularization of Intelligent Information Systems

The conceptual framework of the open intelligent information system architecture allows for the effective partitioning of the knowledge base of an intelligent system. Partitioning of the knowledge base is essential for the effective development of intelligent systems due to the ever increasing size of the knowledge that needs to be represented. Using the modified version of the speech act theory of language (message acts), the open intelligent information systems conceptual framework utilizes a natural mechanism (language) for achieving this partitioning. This use of natural language constructs could also lead to similar approaches where other natural language constructs could be used for distributing complex systems. In other words, attempts should be made to determine what natural language constructs could be utilized for partitioning and integrating distributed intelligent systems.

6.1.5 Integrate Existing Intelligent Systems within Open-World Environment

The implementation of the architecture provides the opportunity and the framework for integrating existing dispersed conventional intelligent systems into an open-systems framework. This integration can be made possible by the development of a comprehensive "concept dictionary" for all the intelligent systems involved in the environment and the associated "communication dictionary" for their communication. Attempts should be undertaken to explore the possibilities for achieving such an integration, thereby converting the existing "closed-world" thinking into "open-world" thinking.

6.2 IMPLICATIONS FOR FURTHER RESEARCH

The development of the OIIS architecture has varied implications for further research. These implications are outlined and discussed below.

6.2.1 Open-Systems Development Methodology

A major research issue arising from the development of an open intelligent information system architecture is the need for a concomitant open-system development methodology which enables the development of such systems in organizations. The methodology could build upon the architecture so as to ensure its purposefulness. Such a methodology would also provide an integrated set of tools and techniques so that important issues viz. appropriate user-involvement, concept integrity checks, level of modularity desired, etc., could be properly addressed.

6.2.2 Open-Systems Development Life-Cycle

A related research issue along with the need for a developmental methodology, should also be the development of an appropriate system life-cycle for developing open-systems in organizations. The conventional life-cycles may be inappropriate due to their premise of closed-world assumptions. An open-system life-cycle could also provide any concomitant open-system development methodology with the various phases/stages that need to be properly addressed.

6.2.3 Machine Learning Mechanisms for Open-Systems

Machine learning is a discipline of artificial intelligence that is concerned with the incorporation human learning mechanisms in intelligent systems, so as to make intelligent systems closer to the human thinking environment. Inferencing mechanisms in existing systems can have such learning approaches built-in in order to improve the performance and versatility of such systems. However attempts need to be made to develop learning mechanisms in the open-world environment in which there is perpetual inconsistency and incompleteness of knowledge.

6.2.4 Usage of Other Natural Language Constructs

The OIIS architecture utilizes the speech act theory of language for communication purposes. Attempts should be made to transform other natural language constructs for inclusion in the communications dictionary. This will further improve the versatility of the intelligent system during problem solving.

6.2.5 Usage of Varied Knowledge Representation Schemes

The OIIS architecture provides for the existence of varied knowledge representation schemes. It is possible for individual knowledge-modules in the OIIS environment to adopt different knowledge representation schemes, thereby using the scheme that best represents their body of knowledge. However further research and experiments need to be undertaken to devise mechanisms whereby knowledge-modules with different knowledge representation schemes would cooperate and communicate during problem solving.

6.2.6 Handling of Uncertainty

A critical issue for open-systems research is the approach that needs to be undertaken to incorporate and use the uncertainty of knowledge during problem solving. The complication in addressing uncertainty in open-systems arises from the fact that during the communication of knowledge, the uncertainty associated with any knowledge depends on a knowledge-module's own beliefs and assumptions. So the important issue is how will a knowledge-module in the OIIS environment handle the uncertainty associated to any knowledge received from another knowledge-module.

6.3 CONCLUSIONS

The preceding discussion addresses the issues that the open intelligent information system architecture raises for information processing system theory and practice. Although this research is quite substantive in its theory and implementation, it is not without some assumptions and limitations which are mentioned in corresponding chapters. Directions for further research, as suggested above, allow for the realization of new issues created by the development of this architecture, thereby providing a continuum for future work. The major thrust of this research is to start a new phase in systems development, which is based on the open-world assumptions and utilizes the sophisticated fifth generation computing techniques.

APPENDICES

APPENDIX - A

```
/ **************************************** /
/ *    Knowledge Base for Marketing Department    * /
/ **************************************** /
/ * Rule for initiating processing of customer order * /

mkt: order (Cust_Name, Prod_Name, Qty, Dt) <-
    mkt: cust_type (Cust_Name, Type) &
    mkt: order_process (Cust_Name, Prod_Name, Qty, Dt, Type).

/ * Rule for detailed order processing for a new customer * /

mkt: order_process (Cust_Name, Prod_Name, Qty, Dt, new) <-
    prst ('Enter sector of economy for customer -- --') & nl &
    read (Sector) &
    mkt: gen_cust_no (Cust_Name, New_Cust_No, Sector) &
    mact: inform (mkt, acct, new_cust (Cust_Name, New_Cust_No))
    &
    mkt: order_details_entry (New_Cust_No, Prod_Name, Qty, Dt,
    New_Ord_No) &
    mact: inform (mkt, acct, cust_ord (New_Ord, New_Cust_No,
    Prod_Name, Qty, ok)) &
    com: com (prod_ship, KS) &
    mact: assert (mkt, KS, prod_ship (Prod_Name, New_Cust_No,
    Qty, New_Ord_No)).

/ * Rule for determining the financial standing of old * /
/ * customers before processing the order             * /

mkt: order_process (Cust_Name, Prod_Name, Qty, Dt, old) <-
    mkt: cust (Cust_Name, Cust_No, Sector) &
```

```
    com: com (cust_fin_status, KS) &
    mact: request (mkt, KS, cust_fin_status (Cust_No, Type)) &
    mkt: order_process_old_cust (Cust_Name, Cust_No, Prod_Name,
    Qty, Dt, Type).

/ * Rule for processing order for old customers with good * /
/ * financial standing                                     * /

    mkt: order_process_old_cust (Cust_Name, Cust_No, Prod_Name,
    Qty, Dt, good) <-
    mkt: order_details_entry (Cust_No, Prod_Name, Qty, Dt,
    New_Ord_No) &
    mact: inform (mkt, acct, cust_ord (New_Ord_No, Cust_No,
    Prod_Name, Qty, ok)) &
    com: com (prod_ship, KS) &
    mact: assert (mkt, KS, prod_ship (Prod_Name, Cust_No, Qty,
    New_Ord_No)).

/ * Rule for processing order for old customers with bad * /
/ * financial standing but satisfactory credit status     * /

mkt: order_process_old_cust (Cust_Name, Cust_No, Prod_Name, Qty,
Dt, bad) <-
    mkt: prod_critical_value (Prod_Name, Critical_Value) &
    ge (Qty, Critical_Value) &
    com: com (cust_credit_status, KS1) &
    mact: request (mkt, KS1, cust_credit_status (Cust_No,
    Credit_Status)) &
    ((Credit_Status = ok) | (Credit_Status = good)) &
    mkt: order_details_entry (Cust_No, Prod_Name, Qty, Dt,
    New_Ord_No) &
    mact: inform (mkt, acct, cust_ord (New_Ord_No, Cust_No,
    Prod_Name, Qty, risk)) &
    com: com (prod_ship, KS2) &
    mact: assert (mkt, KS2, prod_ ship (Prod_Name, Cust_No, Qty,
    New_Ord_No)).

/ * Rule for rejecting old customer order due to bad * /
/ * financial standing and low level of volume       * /

mkt: order_process_old_cust (Cust_Name, Cust _No, Prod_Name, Qty,
```

```
Dt, bad) <-
      mkt: prod_critical_value (Prod_Name, Critical_Value) &
      lt (Qty, Critical_Value) &
      prst ('Customer finances not good.') & nl &
      prst ('Pre-payment necessary to process order.') & nl.

/ * Rules for determining old or new customers       * /

mkt: cust_type (Cust_Name, Type) <-
      mkt: cust (Cust_Name, No, Sector) &
      Type = old.

mkt: cust_type (Cust_Name, Type) <-
      ^ mkt: cust (Cust_Name, No, Sector) &
      Type = new.

/ * Rule for generating the customer number for a new * /
/ * customer                                           * /

mkt: gen_cust_no (Cust_Name, New_Cust_No, Sector) <-
      delax (mkt: last_cust_no (No)) &
      sum (No, 1, New_Cust_No) &
      addax (mkt: last_cust_No (New_Cust_No)) &
      addax (mkt: cust (Cust_Name, New_Cust_No, Sector)).

/ * Rule for entering details of an order in the database * /

mkt: order_details_entry (Cust_No, Prod_Name, Qty, Dt, New_Ord_
No) <-
      delax (mkt: last_ord_no (No 1)) &
      sum (No 1, 1, New_Ord_No) &
      addax (mkt: last_ord_No (New_Ord_No)) &
      addax (mkt: order-detail (Cust_No, New_Ord_No, Prod_Name,
      Qty, Dt, normal)).

/ * Rule for increasing the priority of a pending order * /

mkt: order_priority_increase (Prod_Name, Cust_No, Ord_No, Qty) <-
      mkt: cust_imp (Cust_No, Qty, Imp) &
      (Imp = high | Imp = very_high) &
      mkt: order_pending (Prod_Name, Cust_No, Qty, Ord_No,
```

```
      normal) &
      com: com (order_prior_chg, KS) &
      mact: assert (mkt, KS, order_prior_chg (Pro_Name, Cust_No,
      Qty, Ord_No, high)).

/ * Rule for determining the importance of a customer * /

mkt: cust_imp (Cust_No, Qty, Imp) <-
      ge (Qty, 50) &
      mkt: cust (Name, Cust_No, z) &
      Imp = high.

/ * Rule of rejecting order due to bad credit status  * /
/ * of a customer                                      * /

mkt: cust_credit_standing (Cust_No, Ord_No, bad) <-
      mkt: cust_credit_status (Cust_No, Ord_No, bad) &
      delax (mkt: order_detail (Cust_No, Ord_No, X1, X2, X3, normal))
      &
      addax (mkt: order_detail (Cust_No, Ord_No, X1, X2, X3, pendg))
      &
      prst ('Customer credit standing bad.') & nl &
      prst ('Advance payment necessary.') & nl.

/ * Database of customer information              * /

mkt: cust (john, 21, x).
mkt: cust (jack, 22, y).
mkt: cust (jackie, 23, y).
mkt: cust (mary, 24, z).

/ * Information on the last generated customer number * /
/ * and order number                                   * /

mkt: last_cust_No (24).
mkt: last_ord_No (30).

/ * Database of order details                          * /

mkt: order_detail (21, 25, prod1, 15, 2/15/75, normal).
mkt: order_detail (22, 26, prod2, 20, 3/15/76, normal).
mkt: order_detail (23, 27, prod3, 25, 2/18/80, normal).
mkt: order_detail (24, 28, prod1, 35, 3/12/86, normal).
```

```
mkt: order_detail (21, 29, prod2, 25, 4/12/86, normal).
mkt: order_detail (22, 30, prod3, 45, 5/12/86, normal).

/ * Database of critical quantities for various products * /

mkt: prod_critical_value (prod1, 5).
mkt: prod_critical_value (prod2, 10).
mkt: prod_critical_value (prod3, 12).

/ ******************************************* /
/ *     Knowledge Base for Inventory Department     * /
/ ******************************************* /

/ * Rule for processing the shipment of an order * /
/ * with available product stocks in inventory    * /

inv: prod_ship (Prod_Name, Cust_No, Qty, Ord_No) <-
      inv: prod_stock (Prod_Name, Qty_Bal) &
      ge (Qty_Bal, Qty) &
      delax (inv: prod_stock (Prod_Name, Qty_Bal)) &
      diff (Qty_Bal, Qty, Tl) &
      addax (inv: prod_stock (Prod_Name, Tl)) &
      inv: prod_load (Prod_Name, Cust_No, Qty, Ord_No, Dt_Send)
      &
      mact: inform (inv, mkt, order_shipped (Ord_No, Cust_No,
      Dt_Sens)) &
      mact: inform (inv, acct, order_shipped (Ord_No, Cust_No,
      Dt_Send)).

/ * Rule for processing the shipment of an order * /
/ * with non-availability of product stocks        * /

inv: prod_ship (Prod_Name, Cust_No, Qty, Ord_No) <-
      inv: prod_stock (Prod_Name, Qty_Bal) &
      lt (Qty_Bal, Qty) &
      addax (inv: order_pending (Prod_Name, Cust_No, Qty, Ord_No,
      normal)) &
      mact: inform (inv, mkt, order_pending (Prod_Name, Cust_No,
      Qty, Ord_No, normal)).
```

```
/ * Rule for final loading of the order          * /

inv: prod_load (Prod_Name, Cust_No, Qty, Ord_No, Dt_Send) <-
      write ('Enter Date Shipped') &
      read (Dt_Send).

/ * Rule for changing the priority level of a    * /
/ * pending order                                * /

inv: order_prior_chg (Prod_Name, Cust_No, Qty, Ord_No, Prior) <-
      delax (inv: order_pending (Prod_Name, Cust_No, Qty, Ord_No,
      Old_Prior)) &
      addax (inv: order_pending (Prod_Name, Cust_No, Qty, Ord_No,
      Prior)) &
      prst ('Order placed on high priority pending. Order No : ') &
      write (Ord_No).

/ * Database of various product quantities in inventory * /

inv: prod_stock (prod1, 120).
inv: prod_stock (prod2, 120).
inv: prod_stock (prod3, 20).

/ ****************************************** /
/ *     Knowledge Base for Accounting Department     * /
/ ****************************************** /
/ * Rule for generating credit limits for new customers * /

acct: gen_credit_limits (Cust_Name, New_Cust_No) <-
      acct: new_cust (Cust_Name, New_Cust_No) &
      prst ('Enter lower credit limit for ') &
      prst (Cust_Name) & nl &
      read (Low_Limit) &
      prst ('Enter upper credit limit for ') &
      prst (Cust_Name) & nl &
      read (Upper_Limit) &
      addax (acct: credit_limit (New_Cust_No, Low_Limit,
      Upper_Limit)).

/ * Rules for determining the good or bad financial status        * /
/ * of existing customers regarding previous order payments * /

acct: cust_fin_status (Cust_No, good) <-
```

```
    acct: unpaid_bal (Cust_No, 0).
acct: cust_fin_status (Cust_No, bad) <-
    acct: unpaid_bal (Cust_No, 1).

/ * Rules for determining the credit status of customers * /

acct: cust_credit_status (Cust_No, Credit_Status) <-
    acct: credit_limit (Cust_No, Low_Limit, Upper_Limit) &
    acct: unpaid_bal (Cust_No, Bal_Status) &
    Bal_Status = 1 & le (Low_Limit, 200) &
    Credit_Status = ok.
acct: cust_credit_status (Cust_No, Credit_Status) <-
    acct: credit_limit (Cust_No, Low_Limit, Upper_Limit) &
    acct: unpaid_bal (Cust_No, Bal_Status) &
    Bal_Status = 1 & ge (Low_Limit, 200) &
    Credit_Status = good.

acct: cust_credit_status (Cust_No, Credit_Status) <-
    acct: cust_ord (Ord_No, Cust_No, Prod_Name, Qty, Type) &
    acct: credit_limit (Cust_No, Low_Limit, Upper_Limit) &
    diff (Upper_Limit, Low_Limit, T1) &
    lt (Tl, 200) & Credit_Status = bad &
    mact: inform (acct, mkt, cust_credit_status (Cust_No, Ord_No,
    bad).

/ * Rule for completing accounting details of a shipped * /
/ * and loaded order                                     * /

acct: acct_ord_ship (Ord_No, Cust_No, Dt_Send) <-
    acct: cust_ord (Ord_No, Cust_No, Prod_Name, Qty, Type) &
    acct: order_shipped (Ord_No, Cust_No, Dt_Send) &
    addax (acct: acct_detail (Ord_No, Cust_No, Prod_Name, Qty,
    Dt_Send)) &
    addax (acct: unpaid_bal (Cust_No, 0)) &
    prst ('Invoice Send for Order No - ') &
    write (Ord_No).


/ * Database of customer account details of an order * /

acct: acct_detail (25, 21, prod1, 15, 3/15/75).
acct: acct_detail (26, 22, prod2, 20, 4/15/76).
```

```
acct: acct_detail (27, 23, prod3, 25, 3/18/80).
acct: acct_detail (28, 24, prod1, 35, 4/12/86).
acct: acct_detail (29, 21, prod2, 25, 6/15/86).
acct: acct_detail (30, 22, prod3, 45, 8/25/86).

/ * Database of customers credit limits   * /

acct: credit_limit (21, 500, 1500).
acct: credit_limit (22, 100, 500).
acct: credit_limit (23, 700, 2200).
acct: credit_limit (24, 250, 500).

/ * Database of unpaid balances by customers for previous orders * /

acct: unpaid_bal (21, 0).
acct: unpaid_bal (22, 1).
acct: unpaid_bal (23, 0).
acct: unpaid_bal (24, 1).

/ ******************************************* /
/ *              Concept - Dictionary            * /
/ ******************************************* /

com: com (order, mkt).
com: com (cust_status, mkt).
com: com (cust_fin_status, acct).
com: com (prod_ship, inv).
com: com (order_prior_chg, inv).
com: com (acct_ord_ship, acct).
com: com (cust_credit_status, acct).
com: com (gen_cust_no, mkt).

/ **************************************************** /
/ *  Communications-Dictionary (Message Acts)    * /
/ **************************************************** /

mact: request (Speaker, Hearer, Action) <-
      call (Hearer: Action).

mact: assert (Speaker, Hearer, Action) <-
      call (Hearer: Action).
mact: inform (Speaker, Hearer, Action) <-
      addax (Hearer: Action).
```

APPENDIX - B

WHY1.OUT

order (john, prod1, 10, 2/12/88) wasby mkt from
{ cust_type (john, old) wasby mkt from
{ mkt : cust (john, 21, x) is given
 and
old = old is determined
 }
 and
order_process (john, prod1, 10, 2/12/88, old) wasby mkt from
{ mkt : cust (john, 21, x) is given
 and
com: com (cust_fin_status, acct) is given
 and
request (mkt, acct, cust_fin_status (21, good)) wasby mact from
{ call to
cust_fin_status (21, good) wasby acct from
{ acct: unpaid_bal (21, 0) is given
 } }
 and
order_process_old_cust (john, 21, prod1, 10, 2/12/88, good) wasby mkt from
{ order_details_entry (21, prod1, 10, 2/12/88, 31) wasby mkt from
{ delax (mkt: last_ord_no (30)) is determined
 and
sum (30, 1, 31) is determined
 and
addax (mkt: last_ord_no (31)) is determined
 and
addax (mkt: order_detail (21, 31, prod1, 10, 2/12/88, normal)) is

```
determined
 }
 and
inform (mkt, acct, cust_ord (31, 21, prod1, 10, ok)) wasby mact from
{ addax (acct: cust_ord (31, 21, prod1, 10, ok)) is determined
 }
 and
com: com (prod_chip, inv) is given
 and
assert (mkt, inv, prod_ship (prod1, 21, 10, 31)) wasby mact from
{ call to
prod_ship (prod1, 21, 10, 31) wasby inv from
{ inv: prod_stock (prod1, 120) is given
 and
ge (120, 10) is determined
 and
delax (inv: prod_stock (prod1, 120)) is determined
 and
diff (120, 10, 110) is determined
 and
addax (inv: prod_stock (prod1, 110)) is determined
 and
prod_load (prod1, 21, 10, 31, 3/12/88) wasby inv from
{ write ('Enter Data Shipped') is determined
 and
read (3/12/88) is determined
 }
 and
inform (inv, mkt, order_shipped (31, 21, 3/12/88)) wasby mact from
{ addax (mkt: order_shipped (31, 21, 3/12/88)) is determined
 }
 and
inform (inv, acct, order_shipped (31, 21, 3/12/88)) wasby mact from
{ addax (acct: order_shipped (31, 21, 3/12/88)) is determined
acct_ord_ship (31, 21, 3/12/88) wasby acct from
{ acct: cust_ord (31, 21, prod1, 10, ok) is given
 and
acct: order_shipped (31, 21, 3/12/88) is given
 and
addax (acct: acct_detail (31, 21, prod1, 10, 3/12/88)) is determined
 and
```

```
addax (acct: unpaid_bal (21, 0)) is determined
  and
prst ('Invoice Send for Order No-') is determined
  and
write (31) is determined
  } }
  } }
  }
  }
  }
```

WHY2.OUT

```
order (jack, prod3, 10, 3/15/89) wasby mkt from
{ cust_type (jack, old) wasby mkt from
{ mkt: cust (jack, 22, y) is given
  and
old = old is determined
  }
  and
order_process (jack, prod3, 10, 3/15/89, old) wasby mkt from
{ mkt: cust (jack, 22, y) is given
  and
com: com (cust_fin_status, acct) is given
  and
request (mkt, acct, cust_fin_status (22, bad)) wasby mact from
{ call to
cust_fin_status (22, bad) wasby acct from
{ acct: unpaid_bal (22, 1) is given
  } }
  and
order_process_old_cust (jack, 22, prod3, 10, 3/15/89, bad) wasby mkt
from
{ mkt: prod_critical_value (prod3, 12) is given
  and
lt (10, 12) is determined
  and
prst ('Customer finances not good.') is determined
  and
nl ( ) is determined
  and
```

```
prst ('Pre-payment necessary to process order.') is determined
 and
nl ( ) is determined
 }
 }
 }
```

WHY2A.OUT

```
order (jack, prod2, 20, 3/15/89) wasby mkt from
{ cust_type (jack, old) wasby mkt from
{ mkt : cust (jack, 22, y) is given
 and
old = old is determined
 }
 and
order_process (jack, prod2, 20, 3/15/89, old) wasby mkt from
{ mkt : cust (jack, 22, y) is given
 and
com : com (cust_fin_status, acct) is given
 and
request (mkt, acct, cust_fin_status (22, bad)) wasby mact from
{ call to
cust_fin_status (22, bad) wasby acct from
{ acct : unpaid_bal (22,1) is given
 } }
 and
order_process_old_cust (jack, 22, prod2, 20, 3/15/89, bad) wasby mkt
from
{ mkt : prod_critical_value (prod2, 10) is given
 and
ge (20, 10) is determined
 and
com : com (cust_credit_status, acct) is given
 and
request (mkt, acct, cust_credit_status (22, ok)) wasby mact from
{ call to
cust_credit_status (22, ok) wasby acct from
{ acct : credit_limit (22, 100, 500) is given
 and
acct : unpaid_bal (22, 1) is given
```

```
 and
1 = 1 is determined
 and
le (100, 200) is determined
 and
ok = ok is determined
 } }
 and
ok = ok | ok = good is determined
 and
order_details_entry (22, prod2, 20, 3/15/89, 32) wasby mkt from
{ delax (mkt : last_ord_no (31)) is determined
 and
sum (31, 1, 32) is determined
 and
addax (mkt : last_ord_no (32)) is determined
 and
addax (mkt : order_detail (22, 32, prod2, 20, 3/15/89, normal)) is
determined
 }
 and
inform (mkt, acct, cust_ord (32, 22, prod2, 20, risk)) wasby mact from
{ addax (acct : cust_ord (32, 22, prod2, 20, risk)) is determined
cust_credit_status (22, ok) wasby acct from
{ acct : credit_limit (22, 100, 500) is given
 and
acct : unpaid_bal (22, 1) is given
 and
1 = 1 is determined
 and
le (100, 200) is determined
 and
ok = ok is determined
 } }
 and
com : com (prod_ship, inv) is given
 and
assert (mkt, inv, prod_ship (prod2, 22, 20, 32)) wasby mact from
{ call to
prod_ship (prod2, 22, 20, 32) wasby inv from
{ inv : prod_stock (prod2, 120) is given
```

```
 and
ge (120, 20) is determined
 and
delax (inv : prod_stock (prod2, 120)) is determined
 and
diff (120, 20, 100) is determined
 and
addax (inv : prod_stock (prod2, 100)) is determined
 and
prod_load (prod2, 22, 20, 32, 3/16/89) wasby inv from
{ writer ('Enter Data Shipped') is determined
 and
read (3/16/89) is determined
 }
 and
inform (inv, mkt, order_shipped (32, 22, 3/16/89)) wasby mact from
{ addax (mkt : order_shipped (32, 22, 3/16/89)) is determined
 }
 and
inform (inv, acct, order_shipped (32, 22, 3/16/89)) wasby mact from
{ addax (acct : order_shipped (32, 22, 3/16/89)) is determined
acct_ord_ship (32, 22, 3/16/89) wasby acct from
{ acct : cust_ord (32, 22, prod2, 20, risk) is given
 and
acct : order_shipped (32, 22, 3/16/89) is given
 and
addax (acct : acct_detail (32, 22, prod2, 3/16/89)) is determined
 and
addax (acct : unpaid_bal (22, 0)) is determined
 and
prst ('Invoice Send for Order No-') is determined
 and
write (32) is determined
 } }
 } }
 }
 }
 }
```

WHY3.OUT

```
order (alan, prod2, 10, 3/15/88)) wasby mkt from
```

```
{ cust_type (alan, new) wasby mkt from
{ ^ mkt : cust (alan, V1, V2) is determined
  and
new = new is determined
  }
  and
order_process (alan, prod2, 10, 3/15/88, new) wasby mkt from
{ prst ('Enter sector of economy for customer -- -- ') is determined
  and
nl( ) is determined
  and
read (x) is determined
  and
gen_cust_no (alan 25, x) wasby mkt from
{ delax (mkt : last_cust_no (24)) is determined
  and
sum (24, 1, 25) is determined
  and
addax (mkt : last_cust_no (25)) is determined
  and
addax (mkt : cust (alan, 25, x)) is determined
  }
  and
inform (mkt, acct, new_cust (alan, 25)) wasby mact from
{ addax (acct : new_cust (alan, 25)) is determined
gen_credit_limits (alan, 25) wasby acct from
{ acct : new_cust (alan, 25) is given
  and
prst ('Enter lower credit limit for') is determined
  and
prst (alan) is determined
  and
nl ( ) is determined
  and
read (250) is determined
  and
prst ('Enter upper credit limit for') is determined
  and
prst (alan) is determined
  and
nl ( ) is determined
```

and
read (650) is determined
and
addax (acct : credit_limit (25, 250, 650)) is determined
} }
and
order_details_entry (25, prod2, 10, 3/15/88, 31) wasby mkt from
{ delax (mkt : last_ord_no (30)) is determined
and
sum (30, 1, 31) is determined
and
addax (mkt : last_ord_no (31)) is determined
and
addax (mkt : order_detail (25, 31, prod2, 10, 3/15/88, normal)) is determined
}
and
inform (mkt, acct, cust_ord (31, 25, prod2, 10, ok)) wasby mact from
{ addax (acct : cust_ord (31, 25, prod2, 10, ok)) is determined
}
and
com : com (prod_ship, inv) is given
and
assert (mkt, inv, prod_ship (prod2, 25, 10, 31)) wasby mact from
{ call to
prod_ship (prod2, 25, 10, 31) wasby inv from
{ inv : prod_stock (prod2, 100) is given
and
ge (100, 10) is determined
and
delax (inv : prod_stock (prod2, 100)) is determined
and
diff (100, 10, 90) is determined
and
addax (inv : prod_stock (prod2, 90)) is determined
and
prod_load (prod2, 25, 10, 31, 3/16/88) wasby inv from
{ write ('Enter Date Shipped') is determined
and
read (3/16/88) is determined
}

```
 and
inform (inv, mkt, order_shipped (31, 25, 3/16/88)) wasby mact from
{ addax (mkt : order_shipped (31, 25, 3/16/88)) is determined
 }
 and
inform (inv, acct, order_shipped (31, 25, 3/16/88)) wasby mact from
{ addax (acct : order_shipped (31, 25, 3/16/88)) is determined
acct_ord_ship (31, 25, 3/16/88) wasby acct from
{ acct : cust_ord (31, 25, prod2, 10, ok) is given
 and
acct : order_shipped (31, 25, 3/16/88) is given
 and
addax (acct : acct_detail (31, 25, prod2, 10, 3/16/88)) is determined
 and
addax (acct : unpaid_bal (25, 0)) is determined
 and
prst ('Invoice Send for Order No-') is determined
 and
write (31) is determined
 } }
 } }
 }
```

WHY4.OUT

```
order (terry, prod2, 10, 4/12/88) wasby mkt from
{ cust_type (terry, new) wasby mkt from
{ ^ mkt : cust (terry, V1, V2) is determined
 and
new = new is determined
 }
 and
order_process (terry, prod2, 10, 4/12/88, new) wasby mkt from
{ prst ('Enter sector of economy for customer -- ') is determined
 and
nl ( ) is determined
 and
read (x) is determined
 and
gen_cust_no (terry, 26, x) wasby mkt from
```

```
{ delax (mkt : last_cust_no (25)) is determined
  and
sum (25, 1, 26) is determined
  and
addax (mkt : last_cust_no (26)) is determined
  and
addax (mkt : cust (terry, 26, x)) is determined
  }
  and
inform (mkt, acct, new_cust (terry, 26)) wasby mact from
{ addax (acct : new_cust (terry, 26)) is determined
gen_credit_limits (terry, 26) wasby acct from
{ acct : new_cust (terry, 26) is given
  and
prst ('Enter lower credit limit for') is determined
  and
prst (terry) is determined
  and
nl ( ) is determined
  and
read (50) is determined
  and
prst ('Enter upper credit limit for') is determined
  and
prst (terry) is determined
  and
nl ( ) is determined
  and
read (150) is determined
  and
addax (acct : credit_limit (26, 50, 150) is determined
  } }
  and
order_details_entry (26, prod2, 10, 4/12/88, 33) wasby mkt from
{ delax (mkt : last_ord_no (32)) is determined
  and
sum (32, 1, 33) is determined
  and
addax (mkt : last_ord_no (33)) is determined
  and
addax (mkt : order_detail (26, 33, prod2, 10, 4/12/88)) is determined
```

```
}
and
inform (mkt, acct, cust_ord (33, 26, prod2, 10, ok)) wasby mact from
{ addax (acct : cust_ord (33, 26, prod2, ok)) is determined
cust_credit_status (26, bad) wasby acct from
{ acct : cust_ord (33, 26, prod2, ok) is given
and
acct : credit_limit (26, 50, 150) is given
and
diff (150, 50, 100) is determined
and
lt (100, 200) is determined
and
bad = bad is determined
and
inform (acct, mkt, cust_credit_status (26, 33, bad)) wasby mact from
{ addax ( mkt : cust_credit_status (26, 33, bad)) is determined
cust_credit_standing (26, 33, bad) wasby mkt from
{ mkt : cust_credit_status (26, 33, bad) is given
and
delax (mkt : order_detail (26, 33, prod2, 10, 4/12/88, normal)) is
determined
delax (mkt : order_detail (26, 33, prod2, 10, 4/12/88, normal)) - - -
added previously
and
addax (mkt : order_detail (26, 33, prod2, 10, 4/12/88, pendg)) is
determined
and
prst ('Customer credit standing bad. ') is determined
and
nl ( ) is determined
and
prst ('Advance payment necessary.') is determined
and
nl ( ) is determined
} }
} }
and
}
}
```

WHY5.OUT

```
order (mary, prod3, 60, 4/15/89) wasby mkt from
{ cust_type (mary, old) wasby mkt from
{ mkt : cust (mary, 24, z) is given
 and
old = old is determined
 }
 and
order_process (mary, prod3, 60, 4/15/89, old) wasby mkt from
{ mkt : cust (mary, 24, z) is given
 and
com : com (cust_fin_status, acct) is given
 and
request (mkt, acct, cust_fin_status (24, bad)) wasby mact from
{ call to
cust_fin_status (24, bad) wasby acct from
{ acct : unpaid_bal (24, 1) is given
 } }
 and
order_process_old_cust (mary, 24, prod3, 60, 4/15/89, bad) wasby mkt
from
{ mkt : prod_critical_value (prod3, 12) is given
 and
ge (60, 12) is determined
 and
com : com (cust_credit_status, acct) is given
 and
request (mkt, acct, cust_credit_status (24, good)) wasby mact from
{ call to
cust_credit_status (24, good) wasby acct from
{ acct : credit_limit (24, 250, 500) is given
 and
acct : unpaid_bal (24, 1) is given
 and
1 = 1 is determined
 and
ge (250, 200) is determined
 and
good = good is determined
```

```
} }
 and
good = ok | good = good is determined
 and
order_details_entry (24, prod3, 60, 4/15/89, 34) wasby mkt from
{ delax (mkt : last_ord_no (33)) is determined
 and
sum (33, 1, 34) is determined
 and
addax (mkt : last_ord_no (34)) is determined
 and
addax (mkt : order_detail (24, 34, prod3, 60, 4/15/89, normal)) is
determined
 }
 and
inform (mkt, acct, cust_ord (34, 24, prod3, 60, risk)) wasby mact from
{ addax (acct : cust_ord (34, 24, prod3, 60, risk)) is determined
cust_credit_status (24, good) wasby acct from
{ acct : credit_limit (24, 250, 500) is given
 and
acct : unpaid_bal (24, 1) is given
 and
1 = 1 is determined
 and
ge (250, 2000) is determined
 and
good = good is determined
 } }
 and
com : com (prod_ship, inv) is given
 and
assert (mkt, inv, prod_ship (prod3, 24, 60, 34)) wasby mact from
{ call to
prod_ship (prod3, 24, 60, 34) wasby inv from
{ inv : prod_stock (prod3, 20) is given
 and
lt (20, 60) is determined
 and
addax (inv : order_pending (prod3, 24, 60, 34, normal)) is determined
 and
inform (inv, mkt, order_pending (prod3, 24, 60, 34, normal)) wasby
```

```
mact from
{ addax (mkt : order_pending (prod3, 24, 60, 34, normal)) is determined
order_priority_increase (prod3, 24, 34, 60) wasby mkt from
{ cust_imp (24, 60, high) wasby mkt from
{ ge (60, 50) is determined
 and
mkt : cust (mary, 24, z) is given
 and
high = high is determined
 }
 and
high = high | high = very_high is determined
 and
mkt : order_pending (prod3, 24, 60, 34, normal) is given
 and
com : com (order_prior_chg, inv) is given
 and
assert (mkt, inv, order_prior_chg (prod3, 24, 60, 34, high) wasby mact
from
{ call to
order_prior_chg (prod3, 24, 60, 34, high) wasby inv from
{ delax (inv : order_pending (prod3, 24, 60, 34, normal)) is determined
delax (inv : order_pending (prod3, 24, 60, 34, normal)) -- added
previously
 and
addax (inv : order_pending (prod3, 24, 60, 34, high)) is determined
 and
prst ('Order placed on high priority pending. Order No : ') is determined
 and
write (34) is determined
 } }
 } }
 } }
 }
 }
 }
```

APPENDIX - C

```
/ ****************************************************** /
/ *              OIIS Inference Engine Initiation        * /
/ *                 by predicate 'newexpert'             * /
/ ****************************************************** /
/ * Module transfers processing to predicate 'expert'    * /
/ * Two forms of 'expert' module exist, which are        * /
/ * invoked accordingly. On completion of processing     */
/ * by 'expert' module, printing of the solution         * /
/ * reasoning takes place through predicate 'process'    * /
/ ****************************************************** /

newexpert (Rule: Question) <-
      expert (Rule: Question, Answer) &
      check_track (Status) & cut () &
      dcio (pgmo, output, file, whyshell, out, al, f, 80) &
      process (Answer, Al) & dcio (pgmo, close).

check_track (no_match) <-
      ^ track (match).
check_track (match) <-
      delax (track (match)).

/ ****************************************************** /
/ * Rule for initiating the EXPERT shell of a knowledge system  * /
/ * with no previous reasoning list. This means that the        * /
/ * particular knowledge system is being invoked the first      * /
/ * time. This module then transfers processing to various      * /
/ * 'explore' predicates (having three arguments) for handling  * /
/ * the details of the knowledge base.                          * /
/ ****************************************************** /
```

```
expert (Rule: Question, Answer) <-
      ^ ans_list (Rule, No) &
      addax (stored_reasoning (Rule, 1, [ ])) &
      explore (Rule: Question, Rule, Answer) &
      delax (stored_reasoning (Rule, 1, Trace)).

/ ********************************************************* /
/ * Rule for initiating the EXPERT shell of a knowledge system      * /
/ * with some previous reasoning list. This means that the          * /
/ * particular knowledge system already performed some work,        * /
/ * and is waiting for some response to its communication to        * /
/ * other systems in the OIIS environment, when it is invoked       * /
/ * again. This module transfers processing to various              * /
/ * 'explore' predicated (having four arguments), for handling      * /
/ * the details of the knowledge base.                              * /
/ ********************************************************* /
expert (Rule: Question, Answer) <-
      ans_list (Rule, No) & sum (No, 1, NewNo) &
      addax (stored_reasoning (Rule, NewNo, [ ])) &
      explore (Rule: Question, Rule, Answer, NewNo) &
      delax (stored_reasoning (Rule, NewNo, Trace)).

/ ********************************************************* /
/          * Printing of the reasoning list for 'Question' in file   * /
/                         * 'whyshell out '                          * /
/ ********************************************************* /

process ([ ], [ ]).
process ([Pred, Head1, Head2! Answer], A1) <-
    ((Pred = wasby) ->
          (writes (Head1, pgmo) & prst ('wasby', pgmo) &
          writes (Head2, pgmo) & prst ('from', pgmo) & nl (pgmo) &
          prst ('{ ', pgmo) &
          process (Answer, A1) & prst (' }', pgmo)) ;
    (Pred = is) ->
          (writes (Head1, pgmo) & prst ('is', pgmo) &
          writes (Head2, pgmo) & nl (pgmo) &
          process (Answer, A1)) ;
    (Pred = and) ->
```

```
        (process (Head1, H1) & nl (pgmo) &
        prst ( 'and', pgmo) & nl (pgmo) &
        process (Head2, H2) & nl (pgmo) &
        process (Answer, A1)) ;
    (Pred = call) ->
        (prst ('call', pgmo) & writes (Head1, pgmo) & nl (pgmo) &
        process (Head2, H3) &
        process (Answer, A1)) ;
    (Head1 = added & Head2 = previously) ->
        (writes (Pred, pgmo) & prst (' -- ', pgmo) &
        prst (' added previously', pgmo) & nl (pgmo) &
        process (Answer, A1)) ;
    (Head1 = already & Head2 = executed) ->
        (writes (Pred, pgmo) & prst (' -- ', pgmo) &
        prst (' already executed', pgmo) & nl (pgmo) &
        process (Answer, A1))).
process ([Answer], A1) <-
process (Answer, A1).
process ([ [ ]! Answer], A1) <-
process (Answer, A1).

/ ******************************************************* /
/ * Details of the various 'explore' predicate modules      * /
/ * providing the Inference Control Strategy of a Knowledge * /
/ * system with no previous reasoning list.                 * /
/ ******************************************************* /

/ * Rule for handling COMMUNICATION-D message acts * /

explore (mact: Goal, Rule, [wasby, Head, mact! Answer]) <-
    ^ Goal = (Goal 1 & Goal 2) &
    ax (mact: Goal, Pred, CN) &
    Pred = (mact: Head<-Body) & Goal = Head &
    delax (stored_reasoning (Rule, 1, Trace)) &
    concat (Trace, [wasby, Head, mact], NewTrace) &
    addax (stored_reasoning (Rule, 1, NewTrace)) &
    explore (Body, Rule, Answer).
```

*/ * Rule for handling existing knowledge base rules * /*

```
explore (Rule: Goal, Rule, [wasby, Head, Rule! Answer)) <-
      ^ Goal = (Goal1 & Goal2) &
      ax (Rule: Goal, Pred, CN) &
      Pred = (Rule: Head<-Body) & Goal = Head &
      delax (stored_reasoning (Rule, 1, Trace)) &
      concat (Trace, [wasby, Head, Rule], NewTrace) &
      addax (stored_reasoning (Rule, 1, NewTrace) &
      explore (Body, Rule, Answer).

explore ((Goal 1 & Goal 2), Rule, [and, Answer 1, Answer 2]) <-
      delax (stored_reasoning (Rule, 1, Trace)) &
      concat (Trace, [and], NewTrace 1) &
      addax (stored_reasoning (Rule, 1, NewTrace 1)) &
      explore (Goal 1, Rule, Answer 1) &
      match_check (Status) &
      ( (Status = match) ->
        (Answer 2 = [ ]) ;
        (explore (Goal 2, Rule, Answer 2))).
match_check (match) <-
      track (match).
match_check (no_match) <-
      ^ track (match).
```

*/ * Rule for 'calling' another knowledge system * /*

```
explore (Goal, Rule, [call, to, Answer]) <-
      ^ Goal = (Goal 1 & Goal 2) &
      Goal =.. [call, Rest] &
      Rest = Hearer: Action & Hearer ==/ Rule &
      addax (ans_list (Rule, 1)) &
      expert (Hearer: Action, Answer) &
      delax (ans_list (Rule, 1)).
```

*/ * Rule for checking with the CONCEPT-D * /*

```
explore (com: Goal, Rule, [is, com: Head, given]) <-
      ^ Goal =:= (Goal 1 & Goal 2) &
      ax (com: Goal, Pred, CN) &
      Pred = (com: Head) & Goal = Head &
```

```
        delax (stored_reasoning (Rule, 1, Trace)) &
        concat (Trace, [is, com: Head, given], NewTrace) &
        addax (stored_reasoning (Rule, 1, NewTrace)).

/ * Rule for verifying a fact in the COMMUNICATION-D * /

explore (mact: Goal, Rule, [is, mact: Head, given]) <-
        ^ Goal =:= (Goal 1 & Goal 2) &
        ax (mact: Goal, Pred CN) &
        Pred = (mact: Head) & Goal = Head &
        delax (stored_reasoning (Rule, 1, Trace)) &
        concat (Trace, [is, mact: Head, given], NewTrace) &
        addax (stored_reasoning (Rule, 1, NewTrace)).

/ * Rule for verifying a fact in knowledge base * /

explore (Rule: Goal, Rule, [is, Rule: Head, given]) <-
        ^Goal =:= (Goal 1 & Goal 2) &
        ax (Rule: Goal, Pred, CN) &
        Pred = (Rule: Head) &
        Rule = =/built & Goal = Head &
        delax (stored_reasoning (Rule, 1, Trace)) &
        concat (Trace, [is, Rule: Head, given], NewTrace) &
        addax (stored_reasoning (Rule, 1, NewTrace)).

/ * Rule(s) for handling built-in predicates within * /
/ * existing of different knowledge systems         * /

explore (Goal, Rule, Answer) <-
        ^ Goal =:= (Goal 1, & Goal 2) &
        ^ Goal =:= (Rule: Head1) &
        Pred (built, Head, Goal) &
        Goal =.. [NHead! Tail] &
        explore_aux (NHead, Tail, Rule, Answer).

explore_aux (NHead, Tail, Rule, [is, Head, determined]) <-
        NHead = =/call & NHead = =/addax &
        Head =.. [NHead! Tail] &
        call (Head) &
        delax (stored_reasoning (Rule, 1, Trace)) &
        concat (Trace, [is, Head, determined], NewTrace) &
```

```
    addax (stored_reasoning (Rule, 1, NewTrace)).
explore_aux (NHead, Tail, Rule, [is, Head, determined]) <-
    NHead = =/call & NHead =:= addax &
    Tail =:= [Rule: Action] &
    Head =.. [NHead! Tail] &
    call (Head) &
    delax (stored_reasoning (Rule, 1, Trace)) &
    concat (Trace, [is, Head, determined], NewTrace) &
    addax (stored_reasoning (Rule, 1, NewTrace)).

explore_aux (NHead, Tail, Rule, [is, Head, determined! Ans]) <-
    NHead ==/ call & NHead =:= addax &
    Tail = [Hearer: Action] & Rule ==/ Hearer &
    Head =.. [NHead! Tail]) &
    call (Head) &
    explore_ext1 (Hearer: Action, Rule_Head, Rule, Ans).

explore_ext1 (Hearer: Action, Rule_Head, Rule, [ ]) <-
    ^ explore_forward (Hearer: Action, Rule_Head).

explore_ext1 (Hearer: Action, RHead, Rule, Ans) <-
    compute (list, RHead, explore_forward (Hearer: Action, RHead),
    [ ], List) &
    explore_extra (List, Rule, Hearer, Ans).
explore_extra ([ ], Rule, Hearer, [ ]).
explore_extra ([RHead! Rest], Rule, Hearer, [Ans 1! Ans 2]) <-
    addax (ans_list (Rule, 1)) &
    explore_ext2 (Hearer: RHead, Ans1) &
    delax (ans_list (Rule, 1)) &
    explore_extra (Rest, Rule, Hearer, Ans2).

explore_ext2 (Rule: Rule_Head, Answer) <-
    expert (Rule: Rule_Head, Answer).

explore_ext2 (Rule: Rule_Head, [ ]) <-
    delax (stored_reasoning (Rule, 1, Trace)).

explore_aux (call, Tail, Rule, [call, to, Answer]) <-
    Head =.. [call! Tail] &
    Head =:= call (X) &
    stored_reasoning (Rule, No, Trace) &
```

```
      ^ explore (X, Rule, Answer) &
      delax (stored_reasoning (Rule, 1, NewTrace)) &
      addax (stored_reasoning (Rule, 1, Trace)).

explore_aux (call, Tail, Rule, [call, to, Answer]) <-
      Head =.. [call! Tail] &
      Head =:= call (X) &
      delax (stored_reasoning (Rule, 1, Trace)) &
      concat (Trace, [call, to, ' [ ' ], NewTrace) &
      addax (stored_reasoning (Rule, 1, NewTrace)) &
      explore (X, Rule, Answer) &
      delax (stored_reasoning (Rule, 1, Trace1)) &
      concat (Trace1, [ ' ] ' ], NewTrace1) &
      addax (stored_reasoning (Rule, 1, NewTrace1)).

/ ******************************************************* /
/ * Details of the various 'explore' predicate modules       * /
/ * providing the Inference Control Strategy of a knowledge   * /
/ * system with some previous reasoning list.                 * /
/ ******************************************************* /

/ * Rule for handling COMMUNICATION-D message acts * /
explore (mact: Goal, Rule, [wasby, Head, mact! Answer], No) <-

      ^ Goal = (Goal 1 & Goal 2) &
      ax (mact: Goal, Pred, CN) &
      Pred = (mact: Head<-Body) & Goal = Head &
      delax (stored_reasoning (Rule, No, Trace)) &
      concat (Trace, [wasby, Head, mact], NewTrace) &
      addax (stored_reasoning, (Rule, No, NewTrace)) &
      explore (Body, Rules, Answer, No).

/ * Rule for initiating the execution of a new rule in existing   * /
/ * knowledge base and also checking whether this rule had        * /
/ * been executed before in the knowledge system so that it      * /
/ * is not repeated                                               * /

explore (Rule: Goal, Rule, [wasby, Head, Rule! Answer], No) <-
      ^ Goal =:= (Goal 1, & Goal 2) &
      ax (Rule: Goal, Pre, CN) &
      Pred = (Rule: Head<-Body) & Goal = Head &
```

```
      diff (No, 1, NewNo) &
      prior_expert (Rule, NewNo, Previous) &
      search_head (Rule: Head, Previous, Status) &
      ((Status = match) ->
       (Answer = [Goal, already, executed] &
          addax (track (match))) ;
       (Status = no_match) ->
       (delax (stored_reasoning (Rule, No, Trace)) &
          concat (Trade, [wasby, Head, Rule], NewTrace) &
          addax (stored_reasoning (Rule, No, NewTrace)) &
          explore (Body, Rule, Answer, No))).

explore ((Goal 1 & Goal 2), Rule, [and, Answer 1, Answer 2], No) <-
      delax (stored_reasoning (Rule, No, Trace)) &
      concat (Trace, [and], NewTrace 1) &
      addax (stored_reasoning (Rule, No, NewTrace 1)) &
      explore (Goal 1, Rule, Answer 1, No) &
      ((concat (X1, [already, executed], Answer 1)) ->
       (Answer 2 = [ ]) ;
       (^ concat (X1, [X2, added, previously], Answer 1)) ->
       (explore (Goal 2, Rule, Answer 2, No)) ;
       (concat (X1, [X2, added, previously], Answer 1)) ->
       (explore_end (Goal 2, Rule, Answer 2)) ;
       (Answer 2 = [ ])).

explore_end ((Goal 1 & Goal 2), Rule, [and, Answer 1, Answer 2]) <-
      explore_end (Goal 1, Rule, Answer 1) &
      explore_end (Goal 2, Rule, Answer 2).

explore_end (Goal, Rule, [is, Head, given]) <-
      ^ Goal =:= (Goal 1 & Goal 2) &
      Goal =:= (Rule: Head) &
      ax (Goal, Pred, CN) & Pred = (Rule: Head).

explore_end (Goal, Rule, [is, Goal1, determined]) <-
      ^ Goal =:= (Goal 1 & Goal 2) & Goal ==/(Rule: Head1) &
      Goal = =/(mact: Head2) & Goal ==/(com: Head 3) &
      Goal =.. [Pred! Rest] & Pred = =/call &
      call (Goal).

/ * Rule for checking whether the new deletion of knowledge * /
```

```
/ * from the knowledge base is actually the same             * /
/ * knowledge that was added in the previous working of      * /
/ * this knowledge system, so as to maintain consistency.    * /

explore (Goal, Rule, Answer, No) <-
      ^ Goal =:= (Goal 1 & Goal 2) &
      ^ Goal =:= (Rule: Head) &
      Goal =.. [NHead! Rest] & Rest = [Tail] &
      NHead = delax &
      diff (No, 1, NewNo) &
      prior_expert (Rule, NewNo, Previous) &
      search_clause (Tail, Previous, Status) &
      ((Status = match) ->
        (call (Goal) &
          Answer = [is, Goal, determined, Goal, added, previously] &
          addax (track (match))) ;
        (Status = no_match) ->
        (call (Goal) &
          Answer = [is, Goal, determined])) &
      delax (stored_reasoning (Rule, No, Trace)) &
      concat (Trace, Answer, NewTrace) &
      addax (stored_reasoning (Rule, No, NewTrace)).

/ * Rule for invoking the working of another knowledge system * /

explore (Goal, Rule, [call, to, Answer], No) <-
      ^ Goal = (Goal 1 & Goal 2) &
      Goal =.. [call, Rest] &
      Rest = Hearer: Action & Hearer ==/ Rule &
      diff (No, 1, NewNo) & delax (ans_list (Rule, NewNo)) &
      addax (ans_list (Rule, No)) &
      expert (Hearer: Action, Answer) &
      delax (ans_list (Rule, No)) &
      addax (ans_list (Rule, NewNo)).

/ * Rule for checking with the CONCEPT-D                  * /

explore (com: Goal, Rule, [is, com: Head, given], No) <-
      ^ Goal =:= (Goal 1 & Goal 2) &
      ax (com: Goal, Pred, CN) &
      Pred = (com: Head) & Goal = Head &
      delax (stored_reasoning (Rule, No, Trace)) &
```

```
        concat (Trace, [is, com: Head, given], NewTrace) &
        addax (stored_reasoning (Rule, No, NewTrace)).

/ * Rule for verifying a fact in the COMMUNICATION-D           * /

explore (mact: Goal, Rule, [is, mact: Head, given], No) <-
        ^ Goal =:= (Goal 1 & Goal 2) &
        ax (mact: Goal, Pred, CN) &
        Pred = (mact: Head) & Goal = Head &
        delax (stored_reasoning (Rule, No, Trace )) &
        concat (Trace, [is, mact: Head, given], NewTrace) &
        addax (stored_reasoning (Rule, No, NewTrace)).

/ * Rule for verifying facts in the existing knowledge base     */

explore (Rule: Goal, Rule, [is, Rule: Head, given], No) <-
        ^ Goal =:= (Goal 1 & Goal 2) &
        ax (mkt: Goal, Pred, CN) &
        Pred = (Rule: Head) &
        Rule = =/built & Goal = Head &
        delax (stored_reasoning (Rule, No, Trace)) &
        concat (Trace, [is, Rule: Head, given], NewTrace) &
        addax (stored_reasoning (Rule, No, NewTrace)).

/ * Rule(s) for handling built-in predicates in the            * /
/ * existing or another knowledge system                       * /

explore (Goal, Rule, Answer, No) <-
        ^ Goal = (Goal 1 & Goal 2) &
        ^ Goal =:= (Rule: Head 1) &
        Pred (built, Head, Goal) &
        Goal =.. [NHead! Tail] &
        NHead = =/delax &
        explore_aux (NHead, Tail, Rule, Answer, No).

explore_aux (NHead, Tail, Rule, [is, Head, determined], No) <-
        NHead = =/call & NHead = =/addax &
        Head =.. [NHead! Tail] &
        call (Head) &
        delax (stored_reasoning (Rule, No, Trace)) &
        concat (Trace, [is, Head, determined], NewTrace) &
        addax (stored_reasoning (Rule, No, NewTrace)).

explore_aux (NHead, Tail, Rule, [is, Head, determined], No) <-
```

```
        NHead = =/call & NHead =:= addax &
        Tail =:= [Rule: Action] &
        Head =.. [NHead! Tail] &
        call (Head) &
        delax (stored_reasoning (Rule, 1, Trace)) &
        concat (Trace, [is, Head, determined], NewTrace) &
        addax (stored_reasoning (Rule, 1, NewTrace)).

explore_aux (NHead, Tail, Rule, [is, Head, determined! Ans], No) <-
        NHead = =/call & NHead =:= addax &
        Tail = [Hearer: Action] & Rule = =/Hearer &
        Head =.. [NHead! Tail] &
        call (Head) &
        explore_ext1 (Hearer: Action, Rule_Head, Rule, Ans, No).

explore_ext1 (Hearer: Action, Rule_Head, Rule, [ ], No) <-
        ^ explore_forward (Hearer: Action, Rule_Head).

explore_ext1 (Hearer: Action, RHead, Rule, Ans, No) <-
        compute (list, RHead, explore_forward (Hearer: Action, RHead),
        [ ], List) &
        explore_extra (List, Rule, Hearer, Ans, No).

explore_extra ([ ], Rule, Hearer, [ ], No).
explore_extra ([RHead! Rest], Rule, Hearer, [Ans 1! Ans 2], No) <-
        diff (No, 1, NewNo) & delax (ans_list (Rule, NewNo)) &
        addax (ans_list (Rule, No)) &
        explore_ext 2 (Hearer: RHead, Ans 1) &
        delax (ans_list (Rule, No)) &
        addax (ans_list (Rule, NewNo)) &
        explore_extra (Rest, Rule, Hearer, Ans 2, No).

explore_aux (call, Tail, Rule, [call, to, Answer], No) <-
        Head =.. [call! Tail] &
        Head =:= call (X) &
        stored_reasoning (Rule, No, Trace) &
        ^ explore (X, Rule, Answer, No) &
        delax (stored_reasoning (Rule, No, NewTrace)) &
        addax (stored_reasoning (Rule, No, Trace)).

explore_aux (call, Tail, Rule, [call, to, Answer], No) <-
```

```
      Head =.. [call! Tail] &
      Head =:= call (X) &
      delax (stored_reasoning (Rule, No, Trace)) &
      concat (Trace, [call, to, ' [ ' ], NewTrace) &
      addax (stored_reasoning (Rule, No, NewTrace)) &
      explore (X, Rule, Answer, No) &
      delax (stored_reasoning (Rule, No, Trace 1)) &
      concat (Trace1, [ ' ] ' ], NewTrace 1) &
      addax (stored_reasoning (Rule, No, NewTrace1)).

/ ****************************************************** /
/ * The following modules aid the working of the various   * /
/ * predicate 'explore' modules in their processing.        * /
/ ****************************************************** /

/ * Rules to transfer all previous reasoning for a particular    * /
/ * knowledge system in a List                                  * /

prior_expert (Rule, 1, Previous) <-
      stored_reasoning (Rule, 1, Previous).

prior_expert (Rule, No, [Previous! Rem]) <-
      stored_reasoning (Rule, No, Previous) &
      diff (No, 1, No1) &
      prior_expert (Rule, No1, Rem).

/ * Rules to check if the current knowledge being deleted      * /
/ * had been added in some previous reasoning of the * /
/ * existing knowledge system -- knowledge consistency.        * /

search_clause (Goal, [ ], no_match).
search_clause (Goal, [H1, H2, H3! Tail], Status) <-
     ( (H1 = wasby) ->
      (search_clause (Goal, Tail, Status)) ;
      (H1 = and) ->
      (search_clause (Goal, [H2, H3! Tail], Status)) ;
      (H1 = is) ->
      (H2 =.. [NHead! NTail] &
         ( (NHead = addax ) ->
           (NTail = [NTail1] &
            NTail1 =.. [NHead2! NTail2] &
```

```
          Goal =.. [GHead! GTail] &
          ( (NHead2 = GHead) ->
            (pred_match (NTail2, GTail, NStatus) &
              ( (NStatus = no_match) ->
                (search_clause (Goal, Tail, Status)) ;
                (Status = match))) ;
            (search_clause (Goal, Tail, Status)))) ;
          (search_clause (Goal, Tail, Status)))) ;
     (H1 = call) ->
     (search_clause (Goal, [H3! Tail], Status))).

pred_match ([ ], [ ], match).
pred_match ([H1! T1], [H2! T2], Staus) <-
     H1 =:= H2 &
     pred_match (T1, T2, Status).
pred_match ([H1! T1], [H2! T2], no_match) <-
     H1 ==/ H2.

/ * Rules to perform a forward search for a knowledge system  * /
/ *  rule that can handle the newly arrived knowledge.          * /

explore_forward (Rule: Goal, Rule_Head) <-
     ax (Rule: Goal, Rule: Goal<-*, CN) & Goal = Rule_Head.
explore_forward (Rule: Goal, Rule_Head) <-
     ax (Rule: Rule_Head, Rule: Rule_Head<-Rule: Goal & *, CN).
explore_forward (Rule: Goal, Rule_Head) <-
     ax (Rule: Rule_Head, Rule: Rule_Head<-V1 & Rule: Goal & *,
     CN).
explore_forward (Rule: Goal, Rule_Head) <-
     ax (Rule: Rule_Head, Rule: Rule_Head<-V1 & V2 & Rule: Goal
     & *, CN).
explore_forward (Rule: Goal, Rule_Head) <-
     ax (Rule: Rule_Head, Rule: Rule_Head<-V1 & V2 & V3 & Rule:
     Goal & *, CN).
explore_forward (Rule: Goal, Rule_Head) <-
     ax (Rule: Rule_Head, Rule: Rule_Head<-V1 & V2 & V3 & V4 &
     Rule: Goal & *, CN).
explore_forward (Rule: Goal, Rule_Head) <-
     ax (Rule: Rule_Head, Rule: Rule_ Head<-V1 & V2 & V3 & V4
     & V5 & Rule: Goal & *, CN).
explore_forward (Rule: Goal, Rule_Head) <-
```

```
    ax (Rule: Rule_Head, Rule: Rule_Head<-V1 & V2 & V3 & V4 &
    V5 & V6 & Rule: Goal & *, CN).
explore_forward (Rule: Goal, Rule_Head) <-
    G1 = (V1 & V2 & V3 & V4 & V5) &
    ax (Rule: Rule_Head, Rule: Rule_Head<-G1 & V6 & V7 & Rule:
    Goal & *, CN).
explore _forward (Rule: Goal, Rule_Head) <-
    G1 = (V1 & V2 & V3 & V4 & V5) &
    ax (Rule: Rule_ Head, Rule: Rule_Head<-G1 & V6 & V7 & V8
    & Rule: Goal & *, CN).
explore_forward (Rule: Goal, Rule_Head) <-
    G1 = (V1 & V2 & V3 & V4 & V5) &
    ax (Rule: Rule_Head, Rule: Rule_Head<-G1 & V6 & V7 & V8 &
    V9 & Rule: Goal & *, CN).

/ * Rules for checking if the current goal had been already      * /
/ *  executed during the previous stored reasoning               * /

search_head (Rule: Goal, [ ], no_match).

search_head (Rule: Goal, [H1, H2, H3! Tail], Status) <-
    ( (H1 = wasby & Goal = H2 & Rule = H3) ->
     (Status = match) ;
     (H1 = wasby) ->
     (search_head (Rule: Goal, Tail, Status)) ;
     (H1 = and) ->
     (search_head (Rule: Goal, [H2, H3! Tail], Status)) ;
     (H1 = is) ->
     (search_head (Rule: Goal, Tail, Status)) ;
     (H1 = call) ->
     (search_head (Rule: Goal, [H3! Tail], Status)) ;
     (search_head (Rule: Goal, Tail, Status))).

/ * Rules for concatenation of two lists                * /

concat ([ ], [ ], [ ]).
concat ([ ], T2, T2).
concat ([H1! T1], T2, [H1! Rest]) <-
    concat (T1, T2, Rest).
```

APPENDIX - D

Student Advising System

This appendix provides the conceptual description of an intelligent system for *student advising* based on the open intelligent information system architecture discussed in the thesis. The advising of students about their studies is a perfect application area for intelligent system development. Many students will testify that wrong or misleading advice has adversely affected their academic careers, delayed their graduation and in a way jeopardized their academic work. Unfortunately, there is a shortage of good advisors and therefore an intelligent system which performs some of the counselling will help considerably.

Before proceeding with the description of the student advising system, the rationale for developing the system is explained along with the objectives of the system. Thereafter the components of the system to satisfy the requirements of the OIIS architecture are identified. Finally the conceptual working of the system is discussed.

D.1 Rationale for the System

The subject of advising exhibits the characteristics that are cited as the main motivation for the use of an intelligent system [Hayes-Roth, Waterman & Lenat, 1983; Kulikowski & Weiss, 1984].

1. Advising is frequently repetitive.
2. There are good student counsellors who have extensive knowledge about their educational institution, its programs and the backgrounds of its students.
3. There are not enough experts. The advising needs of the students cannot be met fully.

4. An intelligent system can give good quality advising as:
   -- a system has much more time and patience than a faculty member/counsellor.
   -- a system will not leave to take a position elsewhere, making its advising ability a permanent feature of the institution.
   -- a system could be maintained more easily.

Also experience identifies that there are many areas in student advising that require professional expertise such as the selection and scheduling of courses, course waiving, course transfer, financial grants availability and initial admission chances for a degree or program.

D.2 Objectives of the System

An intelligent system for student advising will provide an interactive environment with the following capabilities.

1. To offer advise to prospective students on admission to particular degree programs.
2. To provide a complete, updated plan of study for a student from pre-matriculation leading to graduation day, taking account of the time constraints, interests and individual constraints of the student.
3. To assist both the student and faculty in determining the waiving of courses and choice of electives.
4. To assist students with the matching of various grants to their needs and purposes.
5. To assist faculty with the prediction of student needs for courses and with the revision of the curriculum.

As the system will be developed on the basis of the OIIS architecture, the various autonomous intelligent subsystems that will exist in the system and their descriptions are outlined now.

D.3 Framework of the System

The student advising system would consist of the following autonomous intelligent subsystems:

1. Admissions Advising

The system which offers advice to students on admission to the degree program.

2. Graduation Advising

The system which advises faculty/students on the prospects of various students graduating within a degree program.

3. Course-Load Advising

The system which offers advice to students on the optimum course-load to be undertaken.

4. Elective Advising

The system which offers advice on the choice of elective courses to be considered.

5. Grant Advising

The system which offers advice on the availability of various grants and their suitability.

Each of the above autonomous intelligent subsystem is now discussed with respect to its purpose and the general content of the knowledge that would exist in their respective knowledge bases. Each autonomous intelligent subsystem may also interact with conventional databases whenever necessary. Specific database accesses are also outlined.

D.3.1 Admissions Advising

The purpose of the admissions advising autonomous intelligent subsystem is to advise students on the prospects for admission in a degree or program offered in the University. The subsystem's advice and the general content of its knowledge base would be based on the following considerations:

1. Past academic credentials of the student:

- -- Degree/Program details pursued.
- -- Number of credits/courses that could be transferred.

2. Past work experience of the student.
3. Program in which admission is sought:
   - -- Matriculated or Non-matriculated.
   - -- Part-time or Full-time.
4. Program academic requirements (Database Access).
5. Program/University financial requirements (Database Access).
6. Analysis of student interests/background.

It is also probable that instead of having a single admissions advising autonomous intelligent subsystem, the intelligent system for admissions advising could be further partitioned into smaller autonomous intelligent systems as mentioned below.

1. Grad/Undergrad Admissions Advising System.
2. Foreign Admissions Advising System.
3. School Admissions Advising System.
4. Department Admissions Advising System.

The general knowledge base contents for admission advising mentioned above can now be assigned to each of the above autonomous intelligent subsystems. Also the above autonomous intelligent subsystems would now interact whenever necessary during and admissions advising problem solving.

D.3.2 Graduation Advising

The purpose of the graduation advising system is to advise students on their prospects of graduation in their chosen degree program. The subsystem's advice and the general contents of its knowledge base would be based on the following considerations:

1. Students up-to-date course-work (Database Access).
2. School/Department/University academic requirements.
3. Students financial standing (Database Access).
4. Specific program/degree requirements (Database Access).

5. Requirements for electives (Interaction with Elective Advising System).
6. Requirements for course-load (Interaction with Course Load Advising System).

D.3.3 Course-Load Advising System

The purpose of the course-load advising system is to advise students on the optimum course-load that can be undertaken in a semester. The subsystem can also advise students on the feasibility of taking a particular course in the program. The subsystem's advice and the general contents of its knowledge base would be based on the following considerations:

1. Students up-to-date course-work (Database Access).
2. Course requirements for the degree/program (Database Access).
3. Requirements for electives (Interaction with the Elective Advising System).
4. Requirements toward waiving courses.
5. Administrative requirements:
   - -- financial restrictions if any that may suggest a reduced course-load.
   - -- residency restrictions (in-state, out-state, foreign) that may suggest specific number of courses.
6. Analysis of student interests/background.
7. Course pre-requisites by approval of instructors.

D.3.4 Elective Advising System

The purpose of the elective advising system is to advise students on the choice of elective courses that can be taken in a semester. The subsystem's advice and the general content of its knowledge base would be based on the following considerations:

1. Students up-to-date course-work (Database Access).
2. Availability of electives for each major in the degree program (Database Access).
3. Requirements for course-load in a semester (Interaction with the Course-Load Advising System).

4. Requirements for waiving courses.
5. Specific interests of the student along with their background, time constraints, etc.
6. Course pre-requisites by approval of instructors.

D.3.5 Grant Advising System

The purpose of the grant advising system is to advise students on the availability and suitability of various financial grants. The subsystem's advice and the general content of its knowledge base would be based on the following considerations:

1. The availability of various grants and their requirements and specific characteristics (Database Access):
   -- financial requirements.
   -- ethnic backgrounds.
   -- area of concentration.
   -- minority status.
2. Students up-to-date course-work (Database Access).
3. Students existing financial standing (Database Access).
4. Requirements for graduation (Interaction with Graduation Advising System).
5. Any administrative requirement, viz. residency status, earlier grants, etc.

D.4 Conceptual Working of the System

The above specified autonomous intelligent subsystems would interact with one another by referring to the CONCEPT-DICTIONARY entries and would use MESSAGE ACT constructs during problem solving. The user-interface of the overall system would find from the CONCEPT-DICTIONARY the autonomous intelligent subsystem that is capable of handling a user's query/problem and would then hand over the working of the problem to it. Figure D-1 below gives a schematic view of the system from an OIIS architecture perspective.

Most of the communication among the involved autonomous intelligent subsystems would be of the Request message act type. As the

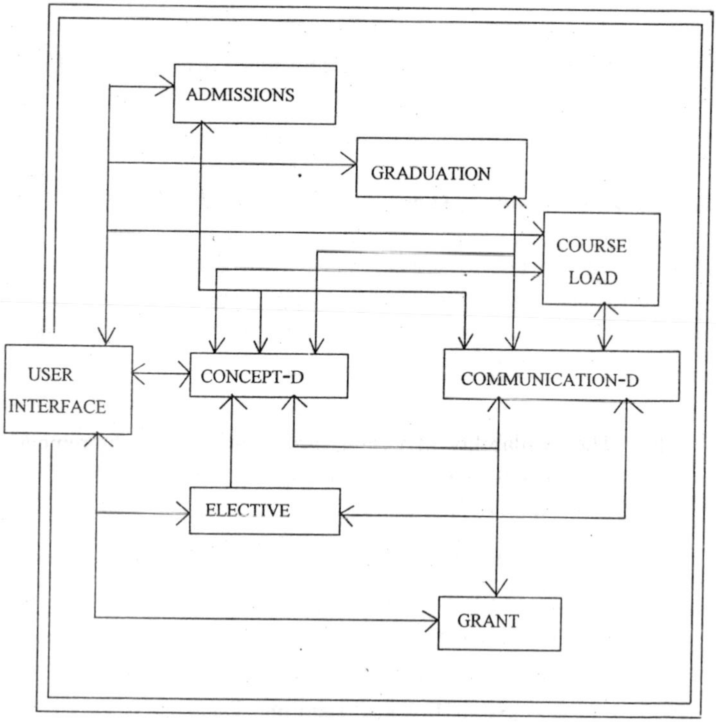

FIG. D-1: STUDENT ADVISING SYSTEM

overall system does not actually perform the operations implied by its decisions (as the thesis case does), few communications would be of the ASSERT and INFORM message act type.

Some of the generic interactions that would take place among the autonomous intelligent subsystems of the advising system have already been outlined in the descriptions of the involved autonomous intelligent subsystems knowledge bases. Other interactions would occur during the further development of the knowledge bases.

The system would be very interactive. Each student's background situation will vary, making the advice given by the system varied. For instance, the system should detect the strengths and weaknesses of students from past performance and adjust the recommended study plan so that it neither overloads nor understimulates the student.

BIBLIOGRAPHY

Agarwal, R. & Prasad, K., ''Enhancing the Group Decision Making Process: An Intelligent Systems Architecture'', Proceedings of the Twenty-Second Annual Hawaii International Conference on System Sciences, Hawaii, Jan. 1989.

Aikins, J.S., ''Prototypical Knowledge for Expert Systems'', *Artificial Intelligence*, Vol. 20, No. 2, 1983.

Allen, J.F. & Perrault, C.R., ''Analyzing Intention in Utterances'', *Artificial Intelligence* 15 (3), 1980.

Alty, J.L. & Coombs, M.J., ''Face-to face Guidance of University Computer Users'', *International Journal of Man-Machine Studies*, Vol. 12, pp. 390-406, 1980.

Attardi, G. & Simi, M., ''Semantics of Inheritance and Attributions in the Description Systems Omega'', Proceedings of IJCAI, Vancouver, Canada, 1981.

Austin, J., *How to do Things with Words*, Oxford University Press, Oxford, 1962.

Balzer, R.; Erman, L.D.; London, P.E. & Williams, C., ''Hearsay-III: A Domain-Independent Framework for Expert Systems'', in Proceedings AAAI 1, 1980.

Belkin, N.J. *et al.*, ''Elicitation Using Discourse Analysis'', Proceedings of Knowledge Acquisition for Knowledge-Based Systems Workshop, Banff, Canada, Nov. 1986.

Belkin, N.J.; Borgman, C.L.; Brooks, H.M.; Bylander, T.; Croft, W.B.; Daniels, P.; Deerwester, S.; Fox, E.A.; Ingwerson, P.; Rada, R.; Jones, K.S.; Thompson, R. & Walker, D., ''Distributed Expert-Based Information Systems: An Interdisciplinary Approach'', *Information Processing & Management,* Vol. 23, No. 5, 1987.

Berztiss, A., ''The Set-Function Approach to Conceptual Modelling'', in T.W. Olle, H. Sol & A. Verrijn-Stuart (eds), *Information Systems Design Methodologies: Improving the Practice,* North-Holland,

Amsterdam, 1986.

Blanning, R.W., ''A Survey of Issues in Expert Systems for Management'' in B.G. Silverman (ed), *Expert Systems for Business*, Addison-Wesley, Readings, MA, 1987.

Brady, M., ''Private Communications'', Working Paper, MIT Artificial Intelligence Laboratory, Boston, 1982.

Brown, J.S., ''The Low Road, the Middle Road, and the High Road'', in P.H. Winston and K.A. Prendergast (eds), *The AI Business: The Commercial Uses of Artificial Intelligence*, MIT Press, Cambridge, MA, 1984.

Bubenko, J., ''Information and Data Modelling: State of Art and Research Directions'', Proceedings of the Second Scandinavian Research Seminar on Information Modelling and Data Base Management, Tampere, 1983.

Bubenko, J., ''Information System Methodologies - A Research View'' in T.W. Olle, H. Sol & A. Verrijn-Stuart (eds), *Information Systems Design Methodologies: Improving the Practice*, North-Holland, Amsterdam, 1986.

Bubenko, J. & Lindencrona, E., ''Handling Object Equality in Federated Databases'', WP129, SYSLAB Internal Working Note, Stockholm, 1988.

Buchanan, J.R. & Linowes, R.G., ''Understanding Distributed Data Processing'', *Harvard Business Review,* July-August, 1980.

Canning, R.G., *Information Systems: New Strategic Role*, EDP Analyzer, Jan. 1984.

Carlson, C.K., ''Knowledge Base Systems Analysis, Design and Development'', Proceedings of TIMS/ORSA Joint National Meeting, Washington, April, 1988.

Cash, J.I. & Konsynski, B.R., ''IS Redraws Competitive Boundaries'', *Harvard Business Review*, March-April, 1985.

Ceri, S. & Pelagatti, G., *Distributed Databases - Principles and Systems*, McGraw-Hill, New York, NY, 1984.

Charniak, E. & McDermott, D., ''Introduction to Artificial Intelligence'', Addison-Wesley, Readings, MA, 1987.

Clark, P.A., *Organizational Design Theory and Practice*, Tavistock, London, England, 1972.

Clemm, G.; Heimbigner, D.; Osterweil, L. & Williams, L., ''Keystone: A Federated Software Environment'', Proceedings of the ACM SIGPLAN Symposium on Programing Languages and Programing Environments, Seattle, WA, May, 1985.

Cohen, P.R. & Perrault, C.R., "Elements of a Plan Based Theory of Speech Acts", *Cognitive Science* 3, 1979.

Corkill, D.D. & Lesser, V.R., "The Use of Meta-Level Control for Coordination in a Distributed Problem Solving Network", Proceedings of the Eighth International Joint Conference on Artificial Intelligence, pp. 748-756, 1987.

Crawford, A., "Some Real-World Issues" in F.W. McFarlan (ed), *The Information Systems Research Challenge,* Harvard Business School Press, Boston, MA, 1984.

Davis, G.B. & Olson, M.H., *Management Information Systems: Conceptual Foundations, Structure, and Development,* McGraw-Hill, New York, 1985.

Davis, R. & Smith, R., "Negotiation as a Metaphor for Distributed Problem Solving", Memo 624, MIT Artificial Intelligence Laboratory, Boston, 1981.

Davis, R. & Smith, R. D., "Negotiation as a Metaphor for Distributed Problem Solving, *Artificial Intelligence,* Vol. 20, No. 1, Jan. 1983.

DeSanctis, G. & Gallupe, R.B., "A Foundation for the Study of Group Decision Support Systems", *Management Science*, Vol. 33, No. 5, May 1987.

DeMarco, T., *Structured Analysis and System Specifications,* Yourdon Inc., New York, NY, 1979.

Dore, J., "Children's Illocutionary Acts", in R.O. Freedle (ed), *Discourse Production and Comprehension,* Ablex, Norwood, NJ, 1977.

Durfee, E.H.; Lesser, V.R. & Corkill, D.D., "Increasing Coherence in a Distributed Problem Solving Network", Proceedings of the Ninth International Joint Conference on Artificial Intelligence, pp. 1025-1030, 1985.

Durfee, E.H.; Lesser, V.R. & Corkill, D.D., "Cooperation Through Communication in a Distributed Problem Solving Network", in M.N. Huhns (ed), *Distributed Artificial Intelligence*, Kaufman, Los Altos, CA, 1987.

Erman, L.D.; Hayes-Roth, F.; Lesser, V.R. & Reddy, D.R., "The Hearsay-II Speech Understanding Systems: Integrating Knowledge to Resolve Uncertainty", *Computing Surveys*, Vol. 12, No. 2, 1980.

Erman, L.D.; London, P.E. & Fickas, S.F., "The Design and an Example Use of Hearsay III", in Proceedings IJCAI 7, 1981.

Evans, M.S., "A Knowledge-based Model of Distributed Problem-Solving", Ph.D Dissertation, The University of Manitoba, Canada, 1988.

Fayol, H., *Administration Industrielle et Generale,* Dunods, Paris, France, 1950 (first published in 1916).

Feigenbaum, E. & Barr, A., *The Handbook of Artificial Intelligence,* Kaufman, Los Altos, CA, 1981.

Feigenbaum, E. & McCorduck, P., *The Fifth Generation: Artificial Intelligence and Japan's Computer Challenge to the World,* Addison-Wesley, Readings, MA, 1985.

Feldman, J.A., ''Structured Neural Networks in Nature and in Computer Science'', in R. Eckmiller and Ch.v.d. Malsburg (eds), *Neural Computers*, Springer-Verlag, Berlin, 1988.

Firebaugh, M.W., *Artificial Intelligence: A Knowledge-Based Approach,* Boyd & Fraser, Boston, MA, 1988.

Floyd, M., ''Expert System Design from a Height'', *Turbo Technix,* March/April, 1988.

Fox, E.A., ''Development of the CODER System: A Testbed for Artificial Intelligence Methods in Information Retrieval'', *Information Processing & Management*, Vol. 23, No. 4, 1987.

Fox, M.S., ''The Intelligent Machine System: An Overview'' in H.G. Sol (ed), *Processes and Tools for Decision Support, Proceedings of a Working Conference*, North-Holland, Amsterdam, 1983.

Galbraith, J.R., *Organization Design,* Addison-Wesley, Readings, MA, 1977.

Gane, C. & Sarson, T., *Structured Systems Analysis: Tools and Techniques*, Prentice-Hall, Englewood Cliffs, NJ, 1979.

Gasser, L., ''Report on the 1985 Workshop on Distributed AI'', *AI Magazine* 8(2), Summer 1987.

Gasser, L., Braganza, N & Herman, N., ''Implementing Distributed AI Systems Using MACE'', Proceedings of the IEEE Third Conference on AI Applications'', Feb. 1987.

Gerson, E.M. & Star, S. L., ''Analyzing Due Process in the Workplace'', *ACM Transactions on Office Information Systems,* Vol. 4, No. 3, July 1986.

Gorry, G.A. and Scott-Morton, M.S., ''A Framework for Management Information Systems'', *Sloan Management Review*, Vol. 13, No. 1, 1971.

Hammer, M. & McLeod, D., ''On database management system architecture'', *Infotech State of the Art Report: Data Design*, Vol. 8, Pergamon Infotech Limited, Maidenhead, UK, 1980.

Hanna, D.P., *Designing Organizations for High Performance,* Addison-Wesley, Readings, MA, 1988.

Harmon, P. & King, D., *Expert Systems: Artificial Intelligence in*

Business, John Wiley & Sons, New York, NY, 1985.

Hayes-Roth, F.; Waterman, D. & Lenat, D., *Building Expert Systems,* Addison-Wesley, Readings, MA, 1983.

Hayes-Roth, F., *Knowledge-based Expert Systems: A Tutorial*, IEEE Computer, 1984.

Heimbigner, D., ''A federated architecture for database systems'', Ph.D. dissertation, University of Southern California, Los Angeles, Aug. 1982.

Heimbigner, D. & McLeod, D., ''Federated information bases - A Preliminary Report'', *Infotech State of the Art Report: Database*, Vol. 9, Pergamon Infotech Limited, Maidenhead, UK, 1981.

Heimbigner, D. & McLeod, D., ''A Federated Architecture for Information Management'', *ACM Transactions on Office Information Systems,* Vol. 3, No. 3, July 1985.

Heimbigner, D., ''A Federated System for Software Management'', *IEEE Database Engineering Bulletin*, Vol. 10, No. 3, 1987.

Henderson, J.C., ''Finding Synergy Between Decision Support Systems and Expert Systems Research'', *Decision Sciences*, Vol. 18, No. 3, Summer 1987.

Hewitt, C. & de Jong, P., ''Analyzing the Roles of Descriptions and Actions in Open System'', A.I. Memo No. 727, Artificial Intelligence Laboratory, MIT Press, Boston, 1983 and Proceedings of AAAI, 1983.

Hewitt, C. & de Jong, P., ''Open Systems'', in M.L. Brodie, J. Mylopoulos & J.W. Schmidt (eds), *On Conceptual Modelling: Perspectives from Artificial Intelligence, Databases and Programing Languages,* Springer-Verlag, 1984.

Hewitt, C., *The Challenge of Open Systems*, Byte, April 1985.

Hewitt, C., ''Offices Are Open Systems'', *ACM Transactions on Office Information Systems*, Vol. 4, No. 3, July 1986.

Hinton, G.E. & Sejnowski, T.J., ''Learning and relearning Boltzmann machines'' in J.L. McCelland, D.E. Rumelhart and PDP Research Group (eds), *Parallel Distributed Processing*, Vol. 1 and 2, MIT Press, Cambridge, MA, 1986.

Holland, R.H., ''The Art of Planning Distributed Databases'', *Computerworld*, April 18, 1983.

Hopfield, J.J., ''Neural networks and physical systems with emergent collective computational abilities'', Proceedings of the National Academy of Sciences 79, 1982.

Huhns, M.N., ''Foreword'', in M. Huhns (ed), *Distributed Artificial Intelligence*, Morgan Kaufman, Los Altos, CA, 1987.

Ives, B. & Learmonth, G.P., ''The Information System as a Competitive Weapon'', *Communications of the ACM*, Dec. 1984.

Jagannathan, V. & Dodhiawala, R.T., ''Distributed Artificial Intelligence: An Annotated Bibliography'', in M.N. Huhns (ed), *Distributed Artificial Intelligence*, Kaufman, Los Altos, CA, 1987.

Johannesson, P., ''Empirical Analysis for Schema Integration'', SYSLAB Internal Working Note, Stockholm, Sweden, 1988.

Johannesson, P. & Wangler, B., ''The Negotiation Mechanism in a Decentralized Autonomous Cooperating Information Systems Architecture'', in G.X. Ritter (ed), *Information Processing 89*, North-Holland, 1989.

Keen, P., ''Interactive Computer Systems for Managers: A Modest Proposal'', *Sloan Management Review*, Vol. 18, Fall 1976.

Keen, P., ''A Walk Through Decision Support'', *Computerworld*, January 14, 1985.

Keen, P. & Scott-Morton, M.S., *Decision Support Systems: An Organizational Perspective*, Addison-Wesley, Readings, MA, 1982.

Kesner, R., *Information Systems: A Strategic Approach to Planning and Implementation*, American Library Association, 1988.

Kimbrough, S.O. & Lee, R.M., ''On Illocutionary Login as a Telecommunications Language'', Proceedings of the Seventh ICIS, San Diego, 1986.

Klein, H., Lander, L. and Ngwenyama, O., ''The Knowledge Acquisition Problem'', Proceedings of the Twenty Second Annual Hawaii International Conference on System Sciences, Honolulu, 1989.

Kobsa, A., ''Knowledge Representation: A Survey of its Mechanism, A Sketch of its Semantics'', *Cybernetics and Systems*: An International Journal, Vol. 15, 1984.

Kroenke, D.M. & Dolan, K.A., ''Database Processing: Fundamentals, Design, Implementation'', SRA Inc., Chicago, IL, 1988.

Kulikowski, C.A. & Weiss, S.M., *A Practical Guide to Designing Expert Systems*, Rowman & Allanheld, Totowa, NJ, 1984.

Laudon, K.C. & Laudon, J.P., *Management Information Systems: A Contemporary Perspective*, Macmillan, New York, NY, 1988.

Lee, D.T., ''A unified method for information system development and database applications'', *International Journal on Policy and Information*, Vol. 8, No. 2, 1984.

Lesser, V.R. & Corkill, D.D., ''Functionally Accurate, Cooperative Distributed Systems'', *IEEE Transactions on Systems, Man and Cybernetics*, Vol. SMC-11, No. 1, Jan. 1981.

Li, Y.P., ''A Distributed Knowledge Model for Multiple Intelligent

Agents'', Ph.D Dissertation, University of California, Los Angeles, 1987.

Lien, Y.E. & Ying, J.H., ''Design of a distributed entity-relationship database system'', Proceedings of the International Computer Software and Applications Conference, Chicago, Nov. 1978.

Lindsay, R.K.; Buchanan, B.G.; Feigenbaum, E.A: & Lederberg, J., *Applications of Artificial Intelligence for Organic Chemistry: The Dendral Project*, McGraw-Hill, New York, NY, 1980.

Lindsay, B. & Selinger, P.G., ''Site autonomy issues in R*: A distributed database management system'', Res. Rep. RJ2927, IBM Research Lab, San Jose, CA, Sept. 1980.

Linger, R.C. & Hevner, A.R., *Principles of Information Systems Analysis and Design,* Academic Press, Orlando, FL, 1986.

Litwin, W., ''A model for distributed databases'', Proceedings of the ACM 2nd Annual Louisiana Computer Exposition, Feb. 1980.

Litwin, W., ''Logical design of distributed databases'', MOD-1-043, INRIA, Paris, France, July 1981.

Luger, G.F. & Stubblefield, W.A., *Artificial Intelligence and the Design of Expert System*, The Benjamin/Cummings Publishing Co. Inc., Redwood City, CA, 1989.

Lundeburg, M.; Goldkuhl, G. & Nilssen, A., *Information Systems Development - A Systematic Approach,* Prentice-Hall, Englewood Cliffs, NJ, 1981.

Lyngbaek, P. & McLeod, D., ''Object Sharing in Distributed Information Systems'', *ACM Transactions on Office Information Systems*, Vol. 2, No. 2, April 1984.

Lyytinen, K. & Lehtinen, E., ''SAMPO Project'', Working Paper WP-3, Department of Computer Science, University of Jyvaskyla, Finland, 1983.

Lyytinen, K. & Lehtinen, E., ''Action Based Model of Information Systems'', *Information Systems*, Vol. 11, No. 3, 1986.

Lyytinen, K., ''Information Systems Development as Social Action: Framework and Critical Implications'', Ph.D Thesis, University of Jyvaskyla, Finland, 1986.

Macdonald, I.G., ''Information Engineering'', in T.W. Olle, H.G. Sol and A.A. Verrijn-Stuart (eds), *Information Systems Design Methodologies: Improving the Practice*, North-Holland, Amsterdam, 1986.

Maddison, R. *et al.*, *Information System Methodologies,* Wiley Heyden, Cichester, 1983.

March, J.G. & Simon, H.A., *Organizations*, John Wiley, New York,

NY, 1958.

Martin, J., *Strategic Data-Planning Methodologies*, Prentice-Hall, Englewood Cliffs, NJ, 1982.

Martin, J., *Managing The Date-Base Environment*, Prentice-Hall, Englewood Cliffs, NJ, 1983.

Martin, J. & Finkelstein, C., *Information Engineering*, Savant Institute Report, Vols I and II, 1981.

Martin, J. & Oxman, S., *Building Expert Systems: A Tutorial*, Prentice-Hall, Englewood Cliffs, NJ, 1988.

Martin, J. & McClure, C., *Structured Techniques: The Basis for CASE*, Prentice-Hall, Englewood Cliffs, NJ, 1988.

Mayo, E., *The Social Problems of an Industrial Civilization*, Harvard University Press, Cambridge, MA, 1945.

McCulloch, W.S. and Pitts, W.H., "A Logical Calculus of the Ideas Immanent in Nervous Activity", *Bulletin of Mathematical Biophysics*, Vol. 5, 1943.

Michalski, R.S., "Theory and Methodology of Inductive Learning" in R.S. Michalski *et al.* (ed), *Machine Learning: An Artificial Intelligence Approach*, Kaufman Publishing, Los Altos, CA, 1983.

Minsky, M. & Papert, S., *Perceptrons: An Introduction to Computational Geometry*, MIT Press, Cambridge, MA, 1969.

Mintzberg, H., *The Nature of Managerial Work*, Harper & Row, New York, NY, 1973.

Mohan, B., *Do Sequencing Rules Exist?*, Semiotica, Vol. 12, No. 1, 1974.

Motro, A. & Buneman, P., "Constructing Superviews", Proceedings of the ACM-SIGMOD International Conference on Management of Data, Ann Arbor, MI, April 1981.

Negoita, C.V., *Expert Systems and Fuzzy Systems*, Benjamin/Cummings Publishing, Readings, MA, 1985.

Newell, A.; Shaw, J. & Simon, H.A., "Empirical Explorations of the Logic Theory Machine", Proceedings of the West Joint Computer Conference, Vol. 15, 1957, pp. 218-239.

Newell, A. & Simon, H.A., "GPS, A Program that Simulates Human Thought" in E.A. Feigenbaum & J. Feldman (eds), *Computers and Thought*, McGraw-Hill, New York, 1963.

Newell, A. & Simon, H.A., *Human Problem Solving*, Prentice-Hall, Englewood Cliffs, NJ, 1972.

Ngwenyama, O., "Towards a Human Action Perspective of Knowledge Acquisition", Ph.D Thesis, State University of New York, Binghamton, 1987.

Nii, H.P., "Blackboard Systems: The Blackboard Model of Problem Solving and the Evolution of Blackboard Architectures", *The AI Magazine*, Summer, 1986.

Nilsson, N.J., *Principles of Artificial Intelligence*, Tioga, Palo Alto, CA, 1980.

Nolan, R., *Managing the Data Resource Function,* West Publishing Co., St. Paul, MN, 1982.

Olson, M., "Knowledge Acquisition for Expert Systems", Proceedings of the Workshop of the Human Factors in Computing Conference, Providence, 1986.

Paradice, D.B. & Courtney, J.F., "Intelligent Organizations", *Texas A&M Business Forum*, Vol. 5, No. 1, Fall 1988.

Parker, C.S., *Management Information Systems: Strategy and Action*, McGraw-Hall, New York, NY, 1989.

Parsons, T., *Structure and Process in Modern Societies*, Free Press, New York, NY, 1960.

Pau, L.F., "Knowledge Engineering Techniques Applied to Fault Detection Test Generation, and Maintenance", in J.K. Skwirzynski (ed), *Software System Design Methods*, Springer-Verlag, Berlin, 1986.

Perrow, C., *Organizational Analysis*, Wadsworth, Belmont, CA, 1970.

Popolizio, J.J. & Cappelli, W.S., "New Shells for Old Iron", *Datamation*, April 15, 1989.

Porter, M., "How Information Can Help You Compete", *Harvard Business Review*, August-September 1985.

Pressman, R.J., *Software Engineering: A Practitioners Approach,* McGraw-Hill, New York, NY, 1987.

Reiss, N., *Speech Act Taxonomy As A Tool For Ethnographic Descriptions*, John Benjamins, Philadelphia, 1985.

Rich, E., *Artificial Intelligence*, McGraw-Hill, New York, NY, 1983.

Robinson, D.A., "A computational view of the oculomotor system", Proceedings of the System Development Foundation Symposium on Computational Neuroscience, MIT Press, Cambridge, MA, 1988.

Rockart, J.F. & Treacy, M.E., "The CEO Goes On-Line", *Harvard Business Review*, January-February 1982.

Rosenblatt, F., *Principles of Neurodynamics*, Spartan, New York, NY, 1962.

Ross, D.T., "Structured Analysis (SA): A Language for Communicating Ideas", *IEEE Transactions on Software Engineering*, No. 1, 1977.

Rothnie, J.B.; Bernstein, P.A.; Fox, S; Goodman, N.; Hammer, M.; Landers, T.A.; Reeve, C; Shipman, D.W. & Wong, E.,

''Introduction to a system for distributed databases'', *ACM Transactions on Database Systems 5,* 1 (Mar. 1980).

Rumelhart, D.E.; Hinton, G.E. & Williams, R.J., ''Learning internal representations by error propagation'' in J.L. McCelland, D.E. Rumelhart and PDP Research Group (eds), *Parallel Distributed Processing*, Vol. 1 and 2, MIT Press, Cambridge, MA, 1986.

Searle, J., *Speech Acts: An Essay in the Philosophy of Language*, Cambridge University Press, Cambridge, 1969.

Searle, J., ''Intentionality and the use of Language'', in A. Margalit (ed), *Meaning and Use*, Reidel, Dordrecht, 1976.

Searle, J., *Expressions and Meaning*, Cambridge University Press, Cambridge, 1979.

Shortliffe, E.H., *Computer-Based Medical Consultations: MYCIN,* Elsevier, New York, NY, 1976.

Sibley, E., ''The Evolution of Approaches to Information Systems Design Methodologies'' in T.W. Olle, H. Sol & A. Verrijn-Stuart (eds), *Information Systems Design Methodologies: Improving the Practice*, North-Holland, Amsterdam, 1986.

Silverman, B.G., ''Should a Manager 'Hire' an Expert System?'', in B.G. Silverman (ed), *Expert Systems for Business*, Addison-Wesley, Readings, MA, 1987.

Smith, R.G. & Davis, R., *Frameworks for Cooperation in Distributed Problem Solving*, IEEE Transactions on Systems, Man, and Cybernetics, Vol. SMC-11, No. 1, Jan. 1981.

Smith, R.G., ''Report on the 1984 Distributed Artificial Intelligence Workshop'', *AI Magazine* 6(3), Fall 1985.

Smith, R.G., *The Contract Net Protocol: High-level Communication and Control in a Distributed Problem Solver*, IEEE Transactions on Computers, Vol. C-29, Dec. 1980.

Smith, J.M.; Bernstein, P.A.; Dayal, U.; Goodman, N.; Landers, T.; Lin, K.W.T. & Wong, E., ''Multibase: Integrating heterogeneous distributed database systems'', Proceedings of the National Computer Conference, AFIPS Press, Reston, VA, June 1981.

Sowa, J.F., *Conceptual Structures: Information Processing in Mind and Machine,* Addison-Wesley, Readings, MA, 1984.

Sprague, R.H. & Carlson, E.D., ''Building Effective Decision Support Systems'', Prentice-Hall, Englewood Cliffs, NJ, 1982.

Sprague, R.H. & McNurlin, B.C., *Information Systems Management in Practice*, Prentice-Hall, Englewood Cliffs, NJ, 1986.

Sridharan, N.S., ''Report on the 1986 Workshop in Distributed AI'', AI Magazine 8(3), Fall 1987.

Taylor, F.W., *The Principles of Scientific Management,* Harper & Row, New York, NY, 1911.

Thompson, J., *Organizations in Action*, McGraw-Hall, New York, NY, 1967.

Tsichritzis, D.C. & Lochovsky, F.H., *Data Models*, Prentice-Hall, Englewood Cliffs, NJ, 1982.

Walker, A., *Knowledge Systems and Prolog,* Addison-Wesley, Readings, MA, 1987.

Waterman, D. & Hayes-Roth, F., *Pattern-Directed Inference Systems,* Academic Press, New York, NY, 1978.

Waterman, D., *A Guide to Expert Systems,* Addison-Wesley, Readings, MA, 1986.

Weber, M., *The Theory of Social and Economic Organization*, Translated by T. Parsons, Free Press, New York, NY, 1947.

Weitzel, J.R. & Kerschberg, L., ''Developing Knowledge-Based Systems: Re-organizing the System Development Life Cycle'', Communications of ACM, April, 1989.

Whitehead, A.N. & Russell, B., *Principia Mathematica,* Cambridge University Press, London, 1950.

Winograd, T. & Flores, F., *Understanding Computers and Cognition*, Addison-Wesley, Readings, MA, 1987.

Yourdon, E. & Constantine, L.L., *Structured Design*, Prentice-Hall, Englewood Cliffs, NJ, 1979.

INDEX

Architectures, 56
    limitation 56
Artificial Intelligence 15, 28, 74
Autonomous Intelligent Systems 61, 66, 69, 75, 78
    Theoritical Foundations, 69
    see also
    Intelligent system

Closed World Thinking 93
Communication Dictionary 85, 93
    Structure 85
Concept Dictionary 84, 93
Conceptual Architecture 14, 92
    Importance, 92
Connectionism 36

Data 26, 47
Data bases 26
Databased Architecture 43
    Composite 48
    Federated 47
Database Technology 28

Executive Support System 24
Expert System 13
Eventual System 26

Files 26
    Indexed 26
    Line Sequential 26
    Random 26
    Sequential 26
Formalisons 36
Formal systems 25

General Problem Solver 32

Information 29
    Engineering 27
    Processing 13, 22
    computerised 22, 13, 22
    Conceptual Architecture, 42
    Manual, 22
    Primitive Concept 42
Information Processing System, 13, 15, 17, 22, 74, 91
    Development 37
    Drawloacks 37
    conventional 17
    Evolution 22
    Modern 22
Information Revolution 13
Information Systems 23, 28
    Advances 38
    Conceptual Primitives 25
    Conventional 28, 40
    Development Methodology 25
    Evolution 39
    Knowledge based 40
    Limitations 39
    Tasks 24
    Types 23, 25
Intelligent Information Processing System 19
Intelligent Information System, 13, 14, 23, 42, 52, 66, 92
    Architecture 50
    Development 15
Intelligent Systems, 18, 92
Intelligent Systems Architecture, 50, 53
Inference Engine 52
    Development 89
    Structure 87
    Knowledge base 51
    User Interface 52

Knowledge 28, 50
Fifth Genration System 16
Information System 15, 74

Engineering 32
Systems, 13, 23, 28, 34, 55
    Advances 40
    Characteristics 29
    Conceptual Primitives 31
    Inference Engine Strategies 32
    Knowledge acquisition 34

Management Information System 24
Modern Information Processing System 22
    see also
    Information Processing System

Neural Network Systems 23, 35, 41
    Evolution 36
    Limitations 41
    Structure 35
Neural Systems 36
    Evolution 36

Office Automation System 15
Open Information Processing System 19
    see also
    Information Processing System
Open Intelligent Information Systems 14, 19, 60, 66, 91
    Architecture 60, 67, 75, 93
    Conceptual Design 75
    Fundamentals 67
    see also
    Intelligent Information System
Open Systems 14, 19, 61
    Approach 60
        Characteristics 60
    Architecture Elements 64
    Development Metholdology 93
    Evolution 61
    Life Cycle 94
    Machine Learning Mechanism 94
    Prospectives 61
Open World Thinking 93
Open World System 91

Perceptions 36
Procedures 27

Serial Processing 41
Software Engineering 28
Speech Acts 92
System logic 28

Theoretical Systems Neuroscience 36
Tractable Formalisms 36
Transaction Processing System 24

Weak Problem Solver 32